STOIC PHILOSOPHY THE RESILIENT MINDSET

Cultivate Peace, Strength & Discipline Through Stoicism for a Life Enriched with Meaning, Confidence, and Intellectual Growth

ALEX HARPER

TABLE OF CONTENTS

INTRODUCTION

Have you ever found yourself overwhelmed by the rapid pace of modern life, where every new day brings a fresh challenge? Whether navigating career pressures, personal relationships, or the constant noise of digital life, there's a profound need for a grounding philosophy that can provide clarity and resilience. This is where Stoicism, an ancient yet remarkably modern philosophical tradition, comes into play, offering practical tools for empowerment in the face of life's challenges.

My name is Alex Harper, and Stoicism has been a beacon during my most turbulent times. Several years ago, I encountered personal setbacks that left me searching for a sturdy foundation amidst the chaos. During this period of darkness and uncertainty, I turned to the wisdom of Marcus Aurelius, Seneca, and Epictetus. The principles they espoused didn't just help me manage my challenges—they transformed my approach to them, fostering a newfound strength, emotional intelligence, and hope for a brighter future.

This book, *Stoic Philosophy: The Resilient Mindset,* is born from a desire to share that transformation. Its purpose is twofold: to introduce you to Stoicism's rich, practical teachings and to offer daily exercises that embed these teachings in the fabric of everyday life. These exercises include the 'View from Above,' a powerful visualization technique to gain perspective; 'Premeditatio Malorum,' a premeditation of evils to prepare for potential challenges; and 'Negative Visualization,' which helps in appreciating what you have by contemplating its absence. By exploring the historical depths and modern applications of

Stoic thought and linking them to practical strategies like those found in Cognitive Behavioral Therapy, this book serves as a comprehensive guide for navigating contemporary challenges.

Structured into thematic chapters, this book explores various aspects of Stoicism, from its historical roots to its relevance in today's personal and professional contexts. Each section combines theoretical insights with practical exercises and inspirational stories, ensuring that Stoicism's wisdom is not only accessible but also engaging. Whether you're an experienced philosopher or new to Stoic philosophy, the content is designed for a diverse audience, avoiding complex terminology and focusing on practical advice that everyone can relate to.

As you embark on this journey, we are pleased to offer a range of free resources designed to support and enhance your experience. These supplementary materials—including detailed guidelines, interactive templates, insightful charts, a comprehensive glossary, and practical exercises tailored to each chapter—can be accessed through the appendix at the back of this book. Crafted to deepen your understanding and help you integrate Stoic principles into your daily life, these tools will enrich your path to personal growth and resilience. I encourage you to dive in and explore these resources to fully enhance your journey.

Unique to this exploration of Stoicism is its broad appeal, demonstrating its relevance across various demographics and its practical applications in leadership and during times of crisis. Moreover, the book respects the integrity of Stoic philosophy while presenting a balanced view that incorporates diverse perspectives within the tradition, including the traditional Stoic emphasis on virtue ethics and the modern perspective of integrating Stoic principles with contemporary psychological practices.

As you turn these pages, I invite you to join me on a personal growth and discovery journey. The exercises and reflections provided are more than just reading material; they are stepping stones to a more resilient and fulfilling life. This is not just about understanding Stoic philosophy—it's about living it.

In closing, I offer you more than just words on a page; I extend a promise that the principles within this book have the power to provide peace and purpose. Approach this text with an open mind and a willing heart, and discover how the age-old wisdom of Stoicism can illuminate your path today, just as it illuminated mine. Welcome to a journey of transformation and hope.

CHAPTER 1

FOUNDATIONS OF STOIC PHILOSOPHY

In a world where change is the only constant, the quest for a philosophy that offers clarity and resilience becomes valuable and necessary. Stoicism, a school of Hellenistic philosophy, has stood the test of time, providing practical tools for navigating the complexities of life with equanimity and poise. This chapter delves into the origins and evolution of Stoicism, exploring its foundational principles and their enduring relevance. From its inception in the bustling markets of ancient Greece to its profound influence on modern psychotherapy and leadership, Stoicism offers a compelling framework for personal and professional growth, with practical applications in areas such as cognitive behavioral therapy and leadership training programs.

1.1 The Birth of Stoicism: Zeno's Influence and Legacy

Origins and Historical Context

In the early 3rd century BCE, a merchant named Zeno of Citium found himself shipwrecked and penniless in Athens. Zeno encountered Socrates's works in a bookstore and was struck by a profound realization of the potential of human reason; this pivotal moment led Zeno to study under the city's renowned philosophers, including the Cynic Crates, who advocated for a life of virtue that was harmonious with nature and free from material excess. By combining Cynic asceticism with the systematic rigor of Socratic philosophy, Zeno created Stoicism.

Stoicism quickly distinguished itself from the prevailing philosophies of the time through its unique approach to logic, ethics, and physics. Zeno's teachings emphasized the development of personal virtue as the path to true happiness, proposing that a life aligned with the rational order of the universe, or the Logos, is the ultimate goal. This revolutionary perspective asserted that virtue alone is sufficient for happiness, a principle that profoundly influenced later Stoic thinkers.

Philosophical Innovations by Zeno

Zeno's philosophical contributions were both broad and profound. He structured his philosophy into three interconnected parts: logic, as a tool for discerning truth; physics, as a way of understanding the universe; and ethics, as the foundation for practical living. His teachings on logic included the introduction of propositional logic, which went beyond Aristotle's categorical reasoning and added depth to philosophical discourse.

Zeno presented a materialistic view of the universe in physics, where everything is rooted in a reason-driven substance he called Pneuma. This concept underpinned the Stoic belief in a deterministic universe governed by divine reason. Ethics, however, was where Zeno's teachings found their most direct application in daily life. He posited that living in agreement with nature requires understanding the laws of the universe and living a life of virtue in accordance with those laws.

Expansion and Adaptation of Stoicism

The principles laid down by Zeno were further developed and refined by his successors, Cleanthes and Chrysippus, who expanded the Stoic doctrine and helped establish it as one of the primary schools of Greek philosophy. Stoicism's appeal grew, and it eventually found its way to Rome, where it became the philosophy of choice among many statesmen and leaders, including Seneca, Epictetus, and Marcus Aurelius.

In Rome, Stoicism took on a more practical form, emphasizing ethical advice and moral guidance suited to the needs and troubles of Roman life. The writings of these later Stoics, filled with compelling ideas on resilience, duty, and the nature of good and evil, have resonated through the centuries and remain profoundly relevant in modern times, offering a timeless guide for navigating life's challenges.

Zeno's Legacy in Modern Philosophical and Practical Contexts

Zeno's Stoicism influences numerous fields today, from cognitive behavioral therapy (CBT) to leadership training programs. In modern cognitive behavioral therapy (CBT), Stoic philosophy is applied by emphasizing that our judgments about events, rather than the events themselves, determine our feelings and behaviors. This aligns with the Stoic notion that our perspective and interpretation of events significantly impact our emotional responses. By helping individuals recognize and reassess their thought patterns, CBT enables them to achieve better emotional and mental health outcomes, drawing significant inspiration from Stoic philosophy.

In leadership, Stoic principles help leaders practice self-control, integrity, and rational decision-making. Modern management philosophies have adopted Stoic virtues, such as leading by example, remaining calm in adversity, and focusing on what can be controlled.

Zeno's teachings, rooted in the belief that virtue is sufficient for happiness, continue to offer a powerful antidote to the challenges of contemporary life. By embracing Stoicism, you are not just learning about an ancient philosophy but are equipping yourself with practical tools for personal excellence and resilience. As we explore these ideas further, you will discover how deeply Stoic wisdom can influence and improve your own life and those around you, empowering you with practical tools that can be applied in various aspects of life.

Year (BCE/CE)	Event	Key Figure
~300 BCE	Founding of Stoicism	Zeno of Citium
~280-206 BCE	Major developments in Stoic logic and ethics	Chrysippus
4 BCE-65 CE	Development of Practical Ethics and Writings	Seneca
55-135 CE	Teachings focused on inner freedom and control	Epictetus
121-180 CE	Reflections on personal and imperial duties	Marcus Aurelius

Timeline of Stoicism

1.2 Key Stoic Virtues: Wisdom, Courage, Justice, and Temperance

The core of Stoic philosophy revolves significantly around the cultivation and embodiment of four cardinal virtues: wisdom, courage, justice, and temperance. These virtues are not isolated traits but are deeply interconnected, reinforcing each other to form a robust moral framework that guides one's actions and decisions. Understanding and integrating these virtues into daily life can profoundly impact how we navigate our challenges and interactions, giving us a holistic approach to life's complexities.

In the Stoic sense, wisdom is the comprehensive knowledge of what is good and evil, what should be selected or avoided, and what is indifferent. It involves the prudent application of knowledge to manage one's affairs correctly and to give sensible advice to others. Practically, wisdom manifests in everyday decisions by applying reason and foresight. Consider a professional facing an ethical dilemma at work, perhaps where company interests conflict with personal values. Here, Stoic wisdom would guide the individual to evaluate the long-term impacts of their decision, encouraging choices that preserve integrity and align with moral virtues over immediate gains. This application of wisdom ensures decisions are not just practical but just and good for all involved.

Virtue	Description	Modern Application
Wisdom	Understanding and applying knowledge appropriately	Making informed decisions
Courage	Facing fears and difficulties with strength	Standing up for what is right
Justice	Treating others fairly and with respect	Promoting equality and fairness
Temperance	Exercising self-control and moderation	Managing desires and impulses

Comparison of Stoic Virtues

Courage is defined not merely as bravery in the face of physical danger but also as the moral strength to stand up for what is right, endure hardship, and face adversity with resilience. For instance, whistleblowers who expose unethical practices in their organizations exemplify Stoic courage by risking their careers to uphold justice and integrity. This virtue is crucial in both personal and professional realms, encouraging individuals to confront rather than shy away from life's challenges, whether in advocating for fairness in the workplace, tackling a public speaking role, or supporting a just cause despite widespread opposition.
Justice involves dealing fairly and equitably with others, ensuring one's actions contribute positively to the community. It emphasizes the importance of treating others with respect and dignity, regardless of their status or relationship to you. A Stoic exemplar of justice, Cato the Younger was renowned for his incorruptible nature and commitment to the Roman Republic. He consistently placed the state's welfare above personal gain, illustrating how the Stoics view justice as integral to social harmony and personal integrity. In modern contexts, this might look like a leader promoting equal workplace opportunities or an individual

advocating for systemic changes to correct disparities in their community. **Temperance**, or self-control, is the moderation of one's desires and impulses. It is about balancing excess and deficiency, which applies to one's emotions, actions, and thoughts. In daily life, temperance can be as simple as resisting the urge to indulge excessively in pleasures like food, drink, or leisure, aiming instead for a balanced lifestyle that promotes health and well-being. It also extends to controlling one's temper in heated situations, allowing for thoughtful and measured responses rather than impulsive reactions.

Relevance of Stoic Virtues in Contemporary Issues

These virtues are not only about personal improvement but are also profoundly relevant in addressing contemporary issues. The Stoic virtues offer a grounding perspective in a world rife with injustice, social unrest, and ethical dilemmas. For instance, in the face of social injustice, a Stoic approach grounded in justice and courage encourages active engagement and advocacy for change, driven by a commitment to fairness and the welfare of others. Similarly, in professional settings, where the pressure to compromise ethical standards can be significant, the virtues of wisdom and temperance guide individuals to make decisions that uphold integrity and consider the broader impact of their actions.

Incorporating Stoic Virtues into Daily Life

Incorporating these Stoic virtues into daily life enriches one's character and fosters a resilient, virtuous approach to personal challenges and professional responsibilities. As we reflect on these principles, it becomes clear that Stoicism offers more than philosophical insights; it provides a practical toolkit for ethical living and leadership in the modern world. By embodying wisdom, courage, justice, and temperance, we can navigate life's complexities with moral clarity and a commitment to the greater good.

By integrating these virtues, we not only enhance our personal resilience but also positively influence those around us. This alignment of Stoic principles with everyday actions prepares us to tackle contemporary issues with a fortified mindset. This brings us to the next essential component of Stoic philosophy: the dichotomy of control. Understanding this principle can further guide us in managing our internal responses to external events, offering practical strategies to maintain our tranquility and effectiveness in the face of life's inevitable challenges.

1.3 Understanding the Stoic Dichotomy of Control

One of the most empowering aspects of Stoic philosophy is the dichotomy of control, a principle that distinguishes between what is within our control—our thoughts and actions—and what is beyond it—essentially everything external. This distinction is crucial, not as a resignation to fate, but as a strategy for focusing our energy where it can be most effective. In Stoic thought, this realization isn't merely theoretical; it's profoundly liberating, guiding us to internalize our efforts on our responses, which are the actual arenas of personal freedom and self-mastery.

Philosophical Reasoning Behind the Dichotomy of Control

The philosophical reasoning behind focusing only on what we can control is closely linked to the Stoic quest for tranquility and virtue. The ancient Stoics believed that distress arises not from external events but from our judgments about them. By adjusting our perceptions and reactions, we align ourselves with what Stoics call 'the natural flow of events,' which is governed by reason and virtue. This alignment is not about passivity; it involves actively and deliberately refocusing on our actions and responses, which measure our character.

Examples of the Dichotomy of Control

Control Examples

- **Within Control:** Thoughts, actions, reactions, decisions
- **Outside Control:** Other people's actions, external events, outcomes

Applying the Dichotomy of Control to Life Challenges

Consider the challenge of a job loss, a situation many of us may face or have faced. The loss itself, including the timing and the fact of the dismissal, lies outside our control and is part of the external flow of events dictated by a complex mix of factors. However, our response to this job loss is entirely within our control. Does one dwell in resentment and bitterness or see this as an opportunity to reassess professional goals and pursue a path more aligned with one's passions? The Stoic uses this moment not to lament the loss but to cultivate resilience and redirect their path towards growth and new opportunities.

Similarly, our control is limited strictly to our responses in interpersonal conflicts, whether in personal relationships or professional environments. You can't control another's words or actions. Still, you can control your reaction—choosing understanding and patience over anger and defensiveness, thereby maintaining your tranquility and possibly transforming a potential conflict into a constructive dialogue.

Addressing Misunderstandings of the Dichotomy of Control

The dichotomy of control, despite its profound utility, is often misunderstood. Critics argue that it encourages passivity or disengagement from societal issues because it suggests that external events are beyond our influence. However, modern interpretations by Stoic thinkers clarify that this principle is not about withdrawal but strategic engagement. It teaches us to engage where we can make a difference—through our actions and responses—and to let go of fruitless anxiety over uncontrollable outcomes. This nuanced understanding is vital in our current era, where challenges—from climate change to social justice—demand personal resilience and wise action.

Cultivating Personal Peace and Pragmatic Engagement

When applied wisely, this concept cultivates personal peace and a pragmatic form of engagement with the world. It teaches us to conserve our emotional and mental energy for impactful actions, fostering a sense of empowerment and purpose. In practice, this means participating actively and passionately in the causes we care about, but without the burden of attachment to outcomes we cannot single-handedly control. This balance is the essence of modern Stoicism—a philosophy not of resignation but of realistic and impactful action.

In embracing the dichotomy of control, we find ourselves equipped with a tool of immense practicality and depth. It allows us to navigate life's unpredictabilities with steadiness and grace, focusing our efforts where they will count the most. Whether in personal setbacks or broader societal challenges, this Stoic principle offers a way to live more effectively and contentedly, grounded in the wisdom of managing our actions and attitudes amidst the inevitable flux of life. As we continue to explore and apply these age-old yet timely teachings, we enrich our lives and contribute to the well-being of our communities, embodying the most authentic expressions of wisdom, courage, justice, and temperance.

Reflection Questions:

1. How do the core principles of Stoicism resonate with your personal beliefs and values?
2. What aspects of Zeno's teachings most apply to your life today?
3. How can you incorporate the Stoic virtues of wisdom, courage, justice, and temperance into your daily routine?

Journal Prompts:

1. Reflect on a recent challenge you faced. How might you have approached it differently using Stoic principles?
2. Write about a time when you acted following one of the Stoic virtues. What was the outcome?
3. List three situations in your life where you can apply the dichotomy of control. How will this perspective change your approach?

CHAPTER 2

DAILY STOIC PRACTICES

In the quiet early hours, when the world has yet to awaken, lies a potent opportunity to set the tone for the day ahead. This time, rich with potential, offers a blank canvas upon which you can paint your intentions and shape your day with purpose and clarity. Stoicism, with its profound emphasis on mindfulness and preparation, teaches us the value of beginning each day not in haste but with deliberate reflection and intention. This chapter explores the transformative practice of morning reflections, a cornerstone of Stoic daily routines that promise to enhance your mornings and the quality of your everyday life.

2.1 Morning Reflections: Setting Intentions with Stoicism

The Importance of Morning Routines in Stoicism

Here are some practical examples of setting virtue-based intentions for the day during morning reflections. By 'virtue-based intentions,' we mean setting goals or actions that align with Stoic virtues, such as patience, gratitude, self-discipline, generosity, and courage.

- Show patience and understanding toward people who are in a hurry, indifferent, or unkind, and focus on responding in accordance with Stoic virtues.
- Practicing gratitude by expressing appreciation to colleagues or loved ones.
- Exercising self-discipline and temperance in handling challenging situations, such as traffic, by maintaining composure and avoiding reactionary behavior.
- Setting the intention to act with generosity and kindness, such as offering help or support to someone in need.
- Embracing the virtue of courage by facing upcoming challenges with a positive and resilient mindset.

These are just a few examples of setting virtue-based intentions during morning reflections and aligning actions with Stoic principles to guide daily interactions and decisions. Other examples could include setting the intention to be mindful and present in all your interactions, to practice moderation in your consumption and desires, or to accept and adapt to the things you cannot control.

Real-Life Examples of Stoic Practice

Marcus Aurelius: As a Roman Emperor, Marcus Aurelius often reflected on his responsibilities and the Stoic virtues required to fulfill them. His meditations are filled with insights on how to handle the pressures of leadership with wisdom and equanimity.

Epictetus: Born a slave, Epictetus overcame immense adversity to become one of the most influential Stoic philosophers. His teachings emphasized the importance of inner freedom and the ability to choose one's response to external events.

James Stockdale: An American Navy Vice Admiral and aviator who was shot down and held captive during the Vietnam War, Stockdale applied Stoic principles to endure and survive years of imprisonment and torture. His resilience and leadership are well-documented and serve as powerful examples of Stoicism in practice.

Tim Ferriss: A modern entrepreneur and author, Tim Ferriss often speaks about how Stoic practices help him manage stress and make better decisions. He regularly incorporates Stoic reflections into his morning routine to set a positive and focused tone for the day.

Stoicism, at its core, is about control over one's internal state, regardless of external circumstances. With its inherent calm and minimal distractions, the morning provides an ideal setting to fortify one's mind against the day's challenges. By establishing a routine of morning reflections, you engage in mindfulness that aligns with Stoic virtues, preparing you to meet the day's demands with equanimity and poise.

This ritual is not about planning the day's tasks but setting a mental and ethical framework to guide your daily interactions and decisions with stoic wisdom and virtue. It's a powerful tool that empowers you to shape your day with confidence and control.

Guidelines for Morning Reflections

The practice of morning reflections can be structured to suit your rhythm and lifestyle best, yet certain elements are essential for fostering a genuinely Stoic start to the day:

Select a Quiet Time and Space: Choose a time and place where you can be undisturbed. Early morning, perhaps at sunrise, is ideal as it offers a natural calmness and a sense of beginning anew.

Meditate on Stoic Principles: Begin with a brief meditation focusing on a Stoic principle, such as the dichotomy of control or the importance of virtue. This meditation can be guided by texts from Stoic philosophers like Marcus Aurelius or Seneca, focusing on passages that resonate with your current challenges or goals.

Envision the Day's Challenges: Consider the potential challenges of the coming day. Imagine these challenges not with apprehension but as opportunities to practice Stoic virtues such as patience, courage, and temperance. Guided by Stoic wisdom, consider the best responses to these situations.

Set Actionable, Virtue-Based Intentions: Decide on specific actions you can take throughout the day to embody Stoic virtues. These intentions should be actionable and straightforward, such as showing gratitude to a colleague, exercising patience in traffic, or practicing generosity with your time.

Examples of Stoic Morning Reflections

To illustrate, let us consider a reflection inspired by Marcus Aurelius, who wrote extensively in his meditations about anticipating challenges with equanimity:

> *"Today, I will encounter people who are in a hurry, people who are indifferent, and perhaps unkind. I will meet this with patience and understanding, remembering that their state of mind is their own and not within my control. I will focus on my responses, ensuring they align with Stoic virtues."*

Such reflections prepare you mentally and morally for the day ahead, enabling you to meet challenges not as disturbances but as moments ripe for virtue practice.

Benefits of a Stoic Morning Routine

When you integrate Stoic morning reflections into your daily routine, you can anticipate a wealth of psychological and practical benefits. This practice enhances clarity and focus, providing a roadmap for how you want to act and respond to the events around you. It reduces anxiety and stress by reframing potential challenges as opportunities for growth and learning, shifting your perspective from apprehension to empowerment.

Practically, a morning routine rooted in Stoic reflection helps improve decision-making and emotional regulation throughout the day. Setting intentions based on Stoic virtues makes you more likely to act consistently with these values, even under pressure. This consistency improves relationships, enhances leadership, and fosters a stronger sense of personal integrity. It's a practical approach that equips you with the tools to navigate the day's challenges with a sense of preparedness and capability, knowing you are ready to face whatever the day brings.

During morning reflections, individuals can meditate on specific Stoic principles such as the dichotomy of control, the importance of virtue, maintaining inner tranquility amidst external events, accepting the things they cannot control, and the transient nature of life. These principles serve as a foundation for cultivating resilience, mindfulness, and ethical clarity in navigating the challenges and interactions of the day. Morning reflections can help reduce anxiety and stress by providing a structured approach to preparing for the day's challenges.

By envisioning potential obstacles and considering Stoic virtues as a guide for responding to these challenges, individuals can reframe these situations as opportunities for growth and learning. This shift in perspective from apprehension to empowerment can contribute to a sense of clarity, focus, and emotional resilience, ultimately reducing anxiety and stress. Additionally, setting actionable, virtue-based intentions during morning reflections enables individuals to approach daily interactions and decisions with mindfulness and purpose, further contributing to a sense of calm and control amidst life's uncertainties.

- Show patience and understanding toward people who are in a hurry, indifferent, or unkind, and focus on responding in accordance with Stoic virtues.

- Practice gratitude by expressing appreciation to colleagues or loved ones.
- Exercise self-discipline and temperance in handling challenging situations, such as traffic, by maintaining composure and avoiding reactionary behavior.
- Set the intention to act with generosity and kindness, such as offering help or support to someone in need.
- Embrace the virtue of courage by facing upcoming challenges with a positive and resilient mindset.

By incorporating Stoic practices into your morning routine, you're enhancing your mornings and transforming your entire life approach. Starting each day with deliberate reflections on Stoic principles equips you to handle whatever comes your way with grace, virtue, and resilience. As you continue to engage with these practices, they transform your mornings and enrich your entire life experience, infusing each day with purpose and calm. This transformation is a routine change and a source of inspiration and motivation for a more fulfilling life. It brings a sense of purpose and calm to your daily life, helping you navigate the day's challenges with a centered and peaceful mindset.

2.2 Evening Review: Assessing Actions and Growth

The stillness that envelops the day's end offers a profound opportunity for reflection and growth. Stoicism, with its unyielding focus on self-improvement and virtue, teaches us the importance of reviewing our daily actions. This practice, known as the evening review, is not merely a ritual of self-assessment but a cornerstone of Stoic practice that fosters a deeper understanding of oneself and one's progress on the path of virtue.

The purpose of an evening review

The purpose of an evening review in Stoicism transcends simple recapitulation of daily events. It involves a thoughtful examination of one's actions, decisions, and emotional responses through the lens of Stoic principles. This reflective process aims to discern not just what one did but why one acted in a certain way, how one responded to challenges, and where to improve. It's about aligning one's actions more closely with Stoic virtues such as wisdom, justice, courage, and temperance and making conscious adjustments to live a more virtuous and meaningful life.

To conduct an effective evening review, find a quiet space to reflect without interruptions. Journaling can facilitate this practice, but even silent contemplation can be equally effective. Begin by recalling the day's events, focusing mainly on moments where Stoic virtues were—or could have been—applied.

Ask yourself several key questions:

- Did I act with integrity and fairness today?
- Was I able to maintain composure in the face of adversity?
- Did I make good decisions, not just for myself but for others as well?
- What could I have done better?

These questions are not meant to incite self-criticism but to foster a constructive critique that encourages personal growth.

Consider a hypothetical scenario where you faced a significant professional challenge, such as a disagreement with a colleague over a project direction. Reflect on how you handled the situation: Did you listen to your colleague's viewpoints patiently and openly, or did you dismiss them outright? Did you find a compromise that respected both perspectives, or did you insist on your approach without considering alternative solutions?

An evening review would involve:

- Analyzing your actions and responses in this context.
- Determining whether they aligned with Stoic virtues.
- Identifying ways to improve your interactions in the future.

The benefits of engaging in regular evening reviews are manifold. Over time, this practice enhances self-awareness, allowing you to become more conscious of your habitual responses and instinctive decisions. It encourages a shift from reactive to proactive behavior, empowering you to choose responses that align with your values rather than being swept away by emotions. This heightened awareness also fosters personal growth identifying areas for improvement leads to better choices and actions in the future

Moreover, the evening review supports greater consistency in living according to Stoic principles. By regularly assessing your adherence to these principles, you reinforce their importance and gradually embed them into your daily life. This consistent practice helps cultivate virtues that define the Stoic way of life—wisdom, courage, justice, and temperance—making them ideals and active expressions of your day-to-day existence.

Through this reflective practice, you learn about yourself and evolve into a person who embodies the Stoic ideal of living in harmony with reason and virtue. As you lay your head down each night, you know you are on a path to better actions and self.

2.3 The Role of Journaling in Stoic Practice

Journaling has long been a revered tool in numerous philosophical and psychological traditions for fostering deeper self-awareness and personal growth. In the context of Stoicism, journaling transcends its everyday use as a diary of daily events; it becomes a dynamic exercise in which you can explore Stoic concepts, reflect on your adherence to Stoic virtues, and track your evolution in applying these principles. This reflective practice enhances your understanding of Stoicism and solidifies your commitment to living according to its teachings.

Writing in a journal allows for a structured analysis of your thoughts and actions, offering a moment of pause to consider your day through the lens of Stoic philosophy. This pause is crucial; it provides a space to step back from the immediacy of daily experiences and view them with an objective eye. When journaling, you are encouraged to focus not just on what happened and how you responded but also on why you acted in a certain way and how your actions align with Stoic virtues such as wisdom, justice, courage, and temperance.

This deep reflection fosters a greater understanding of your motivations and emotional responses, helping you to cultivate a more reasoned and virtuous approach to life.

Guidelines for Stoic Journaling

To engage in Stoic journaling effectively, consider these specific prompts and techniques:

Daily Virtue Focus: At the start of each day, choose one Stoic virtue to focus on. Throughout the day, observe moments when you could apply this virtue, and reflect on these in your journal. For example, if you choose temperance, note any moments of excess or desire you successfully managed or might improve upon.

Challenge and Response Reflection: At the end of the day, write about one or two challenges you faced and how you responded to them. Reflect on whether your responses aligned with Stoic principles and consider alternative actions that could have aligned more with Stoic virtues.

Quote Meditation: Begin or end your journaling session by meditating on a quote from a Stoic philosopher. Reflect on how this quote applies to your current situation and write about any new insights or realizations from this meditation.

Progress Tracking: Regularly, at the end of each week, review your journal entries to assess your progress in living according to Stoic principles. This overview can help you identify patterns in your behavior, track improvements, and pinpoint areas needing further development.

Examples of Stoic Journal Entries To illustrate how you might record Stoic thoughts and reflections, here are example entries:

Virtue Focus (Courage):

> *"Today, fearing criticism, I hesitated to share my ideas during a team meeting. Remembering my focus on courage, I contributed my thoughts and was met with thoughtful consideration from my colleagues. This experience reminded me that facing my fears, even small ones, builds confidence and encourages open dialogue."*

Challenge and Response:

> *"Encountered a rude comment from a neighbor. Initially felt anger, but remembered Marcus Aurelius' advice: 'You have power over your mind – not outside events. Realize this, and you will find strength.' Choose to respond with politeness, preserving my inner peace."*

Benefits of Journaling in Stoicism

Regular journaling in the context of Stoic practice offers several profound benefits. It enhances self-awareness by making you more conscious of how often and how well you apply Stoic principles in various situations. This increased awareness allows for more precise insights into your strengths and areas for improvement, guiding your journey toward greater virtue and wisdom.

Moreover, journaling is a reflective practice that can significantly contribute to your emotional and philosophical growth. By consistently examining your thoughts and actions through the lens of Stoicism, you develop a deeper understanding of this philosophical discipline, not just as a theoretical framework but as a practical guide to everyday living. This practice helps to solidify Stoic principles in your life, making them readily accessible as tools for handling the complexities and challenges of modern existence.

Through the disciplined practice of Stoic journaling, you will likely experience a more grounded and thoughtful engagement with the world around you. This journaling process encourages a life lived with intention and virtue, aligning your actions more closely with the Stoic ideal of a rational and fulfilling existence. As you continue to record and reflect upon your daily experiences, the pages of your journal bear witness to a life enriched by philosophy and guided by the timeless wisdom of Stoicism.

As we close this chapter, remember that each entry in your Stoic journal is more than just a record; it is a step towards a deeper understanding of yourself and your path through the Stoic virtues. This practice is an invitation to continually evolve, question, and grow through external achievements and the internal cultivation of wisdom, justice, courage, and temperance. Let your journal be a mirror and map, reflecting who you are and guiding your aspirations.

For detailed guidelines and examples of Stoic journaling, please refer to the free resources mentioned at the start of the book.

Reflection Questions:

1. How can establishing a morning routine enhance your ability to practice Stoicism throughout the day?

2. What are some potential obstacles to maintaining a Stoic daily routine, and how can you overcome them?
3. How does reflecting on your actions at the end of the day help you grow in virtue?

Journal Prompts:

1. Outline your ideal morning routine incorporating Stoic reflections and meditations.
2. Write about a specific event where you succeeded in applying Stoic principles. What did you learn from this experience?
3. Create a weekly plan that includes time for both morning reflections and evening reviews. How do you feel after following this plan for a week?

CHAPTER 3

STOICISM AND MODERN PSYCHOLOGY

In the rich tapestry of philosophical thought and psychological practice, few intersections are as profound and practical as between Stoicism and Cognitive Behavioral Therapy (CBT). As you navigate the complexities of modern life, understanding this alignment offers insight and actionable strategies to manage psychological challenges. Stoicism, focusing on rational control of one's emotions and actions, provides a philosophical backbone to many contemporary therapeutic practices, particularly CBT. This chapter explores how these ancient principles, when applied in modern life, can empower individuals to cultivate mental resilience and emotional clarity, giving them a sense of control over their psychological well-being.

3.1 Stoicism & CBT: A Practical Alignment

Foundational Similarities between Stoicism and CBT

At the heart of both Stoicism and Cognitive Behavioral Therapy lies a fundamental emphasis on the importance of perception in shaping our emotional and behavioral responses. Stoicism teaches that events do not disturb people but rather their judgments about those events. This Stoic axiom mirrors the central premise of CBT, which posits that psychological distress is primarily a result of cognitive appraisal rather than external circumstances. Both philosophies advocate for a shift in mental frameworks to alter emotional states and behaviors, suggesting that profound control over one's mental health lies in the mastery of one's thoughts.

CBT, developed in the mid-20th century, incorporates a variety of techniques aimed at changing maladaptive thinking patterns that lead to emotional distress. These techniques are deeply reminiscent of Stoic practices. For instance, the Stoic exercise of challenging assumptions and reframing thoughts to align more closely with reality. Additional practical exercises that blend Stoicism and CBT include:

- Journaling about challenging situations from a Stoic perspective.
- Practicing gratitude to reframe negative thoughts.
- Using visualization techniques to confront fears and anxieties in a controlled manner.

This is paralleled in CBT's cognitive restructuring process. This process involves identifying and disputing irrational or maladaptive thoughts and replacing them with more accurate and beneficial thoughts.

This practice echoes the Stoic discipline of assent, where one is encouraged to accept only accurate impressions and dismiss those that are false. In other words, it's about learning to trust your rational mind and not giving in to emotional reactions based on false perceptions. This is a crucial Stoic principle that can help you maintain emotional balance in challenging situations.

Techniques Derived from Stoicism Used in CBT

Cognitive restructuring, a core component of CBT, involves identifying thought distortions and systematically evaluating their validity. This technique is strikingly similar to the Stoic practice of challenging and changing irrational beliefs. Stoics were pioneers in practicing what we might now call cognitive distancing – observing one's thoughts and recognizing that they are separate from the essence of one's rational mind.

For example, Epictetus, a prominent Stoic philosopher, suggested that individuals pause and reflect on their impressions, asking themselves, "Is this something that is within my control?" before reacting emotionally. This reflective pause is utilized in CBT as a moment of cognitive appraisal, where the individual assesses the accuracy and helpfulness of their thoughts before responding emotionally. By integrating these Stoic principles, CBT helps individuals realize that they can choose their reactions by altering their perceptions.

Case Studies Demonstrating the Effectiveness of Stoic-based CBT

Consider the case of a young professional suffering from severe anxiety due to workplace pressure. Through CBT, infused with Stoic principles, the individual learned to identify the catastrophic thoughts fueling their anxiety, such as 'I will never succeed,' and to challenge and replace these with more rational and less absolute thoughts, like 'I have succeeded before and can do so again.' This practical application of Stoic-based CBT significantly reduced their anxiety levels. It improved their overall functioning at work, demonstrating the effectiveness of these tools in managing workplace stress and anxiety.

Another case involves a veteran dealing with post-traumatic stress disorder (PTSD), where CBT techniques based on Stoic principles were employed to help manage intrusive memories and emotional numbness. By applying Stoic mindfulness—focusing on present experiences rather than past traumas—the veteran could gain significant relief from their symptoms, demonstrating the enduring utility and hope that Stoic wisdom brings to modern psychological healing. This enduring utility of Stoic wisdom should instill a sense of hope and optimism in the audience, showing them that there are practical tools for managing psychological challenges.

Practical Exercises Blending Stoicism and CBT

To integrate the benefits of Stoicism and CBT into your daily life, consider engaging in the following exercise, designed to enhance mindfulness and cognitive restructuring:

Mindful Meditation on Control: Meditate on the Stoic dichotomy of control for a few minutes. Focus on distinguishing between what is within your control (thoughts, perceptions, and actions) and what is not (external events, other people's actions). This meditation grounds you in the present moment and sets the stage for cognitive restructuring.

Cognitive Restructuring Exercise: Identify a recent event that caused you distress. Write down the automatic thoughts that occurred when the event happened. Next to each thought, write a more rational, Stoic-inspired response. For instance, if your initial thought was, *"This always happens to me,"* you might reframe it to *"Sometimes, I experience setbacks, but each is an opportunity to learn and grow."*

These exercises are therapeutic techniques and invitations to a deeper understanding of yourself and a more reasoned approach to life's challenges. By practicing them, you cultivate psychological resilience and profound inner peace, reflective of both Stoic wisdom and the therapeutic power of CBT. As you continue to explore these practices, remember that the journey toward emotional and mental well-being is continuous, and each step, informed by the rich dialogue between Stoicism and modern psychology, is a step toward a more fulfilled and rational life. This constant journey should encourage and motivate you to keep moving forward.

3.2 Emotional Resilience: Stoic Strategies for Mental Health

From a Stoic perspective, emotional resilience is the capacity to sustain your core stability and persist in functioning effectively, regardless of emotional challenges. This resilience is pivotal, not as a mere resistance to emotional pain, but as an active, dynamic capability to process and recover from emotional disturbances.

Understanding and Managing Responses

Stoicism teaches that resilience comes from understanding that we can control our responses to external events, even if we cannot control the events themselves. This philosophy empowers you to maintain a steady course through life's inevitable storms, using rational thinking to manage and mitigate emotional upheaval.

Exercises for Building Resilience

Stoicism offers several exercises that can help in building this kind of resilience. One such exercise is **voluntary discomfort**, where you intentionally place yourself in uncomfortable situations to develop a greater tolerance for hardship and discomfort. Examples include taking cold showers, fasting for a day, or engaging in strenuous physical activity. This practice strengthens your ability to remain composed and make rational decisions under stress.

Another key exercise is **reflecting on adversity**, which involves regularly contemplating potentially challenging scenarios and imagining how you would handle them using Stoic principles. This mental preparation diminishes the psychological impact of real-life hardships and reduces anxiety, increasing your preparedness.

Real-Life Applications

The real-life applications of these Stoic resilience strategies are numerous and profound. In **business leadership**, a leader navigating a company through financial turmoil can mitigate panic and maintain rational decision-making by applying Stoic principles.

For those dealing with **chronic illness**, Stoicism offers solace and strength by encouraging a focus on what can be controlled and finding joy in other aspects of life despite physical limitations.

Comparison with Modern Psychological Approaches

Comparing Stoic strategies for building resilience with modern psychological approaches reveals contrasts and convergences. **Modern methods** often emphasize external support systems, communication of emotions, and professional therapy. In contrast, the **Stoic approach** emphasizes internal resources—reason, self-reflection, and the disciplined control of perceptions and reactions. It encourages confronting and rationalizing discomfort as a path to emotional growth and resilience.

Complementary Strategies

The Stoic approach complements modern psychological strategies by fortifying internal coping mechanisms. For instance, while therapy might help someone understand the sources of their anxiety, Stoic practices like **premeditating adversities** can provide daily tools for managing anxiety triggers. This synergy offers a holistic approach that combines internal fortitude with external support.

As you continue to explore these Stoic exercises and integrate them into your life, remember that the goal is not to suppress or deny your emotions, but to manage them with wisdom and rationality. This approach does not promise an absence of emotional pain but provides a robust framework for navigating through it with grace and strength. By fostering Stoic resilience, you are equipped not only to survive life's challenges but to thrive amidst them, preserving your mental health and contributing positively to your personal and professional spheres.

3.3 Rational Emotive Behavior Therapy and Stoic Thought

Rational Emotive Behavior Therapy (REBT), established by the psychologist Albert Ellis in the mid-20th century, is a pioneering form of cognitive-behavioral therapy. It shares a profound philosophical lineage with Stoicism, particularly in its approach to managing emotions and behaviors through examining and restructuring beliefs. Ellis openly acknowledged the influence of Stoic philosophy on REBT, emphasizing that the distress individuals experience from adverse events is primarily a result of their beliefs about these events, not the events themselves.

Ellis encapsulated the core of REBT in the ABC model, where 'A' represents an activating event, 'B' denotes the belief about the event, and 'C' signifies the consequence, which includes the emotional and behavioral response. This model mirrors the Stoic understanding that it is not events themselves that disturb us but our judgments about them. Stoicism teaches us to maintain tranquility despite external circumstances by changing our perceptions. Similarly, REBT focuses on identifying irrational or maladaptive beliefs triggered by activating events and restructuring these beliefs to reduce emotional distress and promote healthier behaviors.

REBT employs specific techniques that reflect Stoic practices, particularly in disputing irrational beliefs. This technique involves challenging and questioning the assumptions that lead to negative emotions and behaviors, encouraging individuals to replace these beliefs with more rational and flexible ones. The practice is akin to the Stoic method of examining one's impressions to determine their accuracy and whether they should be accepted or rejected. Stoics like Epictetus emphasized that people are disturbed not by things but by the views they take of them, a sentiment that directly informs the therapeutic strategies in REBT.

For instance, if someone becomes extremely upset after receiving criticism at work, REBT would help them identify the belief causing their distress—perhaps the idea that they must be competent in all aspects of their job at all times. By disputing this belief as irrational and unrealistic and replacing it with a more flexible belief, such as recognizing that everyone has areas to improve and that criticism can be a valuable tool for growth, the individual can reduce their distress and respond more constructively to feedback.

One practical exercise involves daily reflection using the ABC model in a Stoic context with REBT techniques. Start by journaling about an event that caused significant emotional distress during the day. Describe the event (Activating Event), identify the belief about the event that led to distress (Belief), and note the emotional and behavioral outcome (Consequence). Then, ask yourself if the evidence supports the irrational belief and whether it is based on unrealistic assumptions to dispute it. Finally, envision how altering this belief could change your emotional and behavioral response to align more closely with the Stoic virtues of rationality and emotional stability.

Integrating REBT with Stoic thought gives you a robust framework for understanding and managing your emotional life and a practical toolkit for daily living. This synthesis empowers you to face life's adversities with a fortified mind, transforming challenges into opportunities for growth and deeper understanding. As you continue to explore and apply these principles, remember that the ultimate goal is not to eliminate all emotional pain but to master your reactions, fostering a life marked by rationality, resilience, and profound inner peace.

In sum, REBT and Stoic thought provide a robust approach to mental health that emphasizes the power of perception in shaping our emotional and behavioral realities. This chapter has explored how aligning Ellis's therapeutic techniques with Stoic wisdom can significantly enhance emotional intelligence and foster a resilient, fulfilling life. As we turn to the next chapter, we will delve deeper into how these time-tested philosophies can be applied to modern challenges, offering further strategies to live with intention and integrity.

Reflection Questions:

1. How do the principles of Stoicism align with or differ from modern psychological practices like CBT?
2. What benefits do you see in combining Stoic philosophy with modern therapeutic techniques?
3. How can Stoic practices help you manage your emotions and thoughts more effectively?

Journal Prompts:

1. Reflect on a recent emotional reaction you had. How could you have used Stoic techniques to manage this reaction?
2. Write about a belief you hold that causes you distress. How can you reframe this belief using Stoic principles?
3. Describe a situation where you successfully used cognitive restructuring to change your perception and emotional response.

CHAPTER 4

STOICISM IN PROFESSIONAL LIFE

The necessity for a stable guiding philosophy becomes evident in the labyrinth of modern professional life, where leadership often succumbs to the pressures of deadlines, targets, and constant competition. Stoicism, with its profound emphasis on virtue, self-control, and focus on the common good, offers a beacon of wisdom that is applicable and essential in contemporary leadership. This chapter delves into Stoic leadership—a style characterized not by pursuing personal glory or power but by committing to ethical behavior, emotional intelligence, and service to others.

4.1 Stoic Leadership: Leading with Calm and Purpose

Defining Stoic Leadership

Stoic leadership, in its essence, is rooted in the pursuit of virtue and the practice of self-awareness and self-discipline. It is a form of leadership that does not measure success by the usual metrics of profit and prestige but by the well-being of the team and the integrity of their actions. Stoic leaders prioritize the development of their character as much as the development of their company's strategy, understanding that the actual value of leadership lies in the example they set and the ethical standards they uphold.

A Stoic leader views power as a responsibility to do good and act justly rather than as an opportunity for personal gain. They lead calmly and purposefully, using reason to navigate the complexities of management and decision-making while maintaining a compassionate understanding of their team's needs and aspirations. This leadership style is not passive; it is actively engaged and deeply committed to fostering an environment where individuals and the collective can thrive.

Examples of Stoic Leaders Throughout History

One of the most iconic figures embodying Stoic leadership is Marcus Aurelius, the Roman Emperor known for his philosophical treatise, *Meditations*. Despite his vast power, Aurelius governed with a commitment to virtue and justice, often reflecting on his responsibilities and the proper use of his authority. His leadership was not free from challenges, including wars and internal strife, yet his writings reflect a continuous commitment to Stoic principles, emphasizing duty, rationality, and the common good.

In a modern context, consider someone like Nelson Mandela, whose leadership, though not labeled Stoic, shared similar virtues. Mandela's focus on forgiveness, peace, and equality in the face of immense personal and political challenges showcases the Stoic ideals of courage and justice. His leadership transformed a nation and continues to inspire leaders around the globe, demonstrating the timeless relevance of leading with virtue and integrity.

Principles of Stoic Leadership in Action

In practical terms, Stoic leadership manifests through several key behaviors:

- **Emotional Regulation:** Stoic leaders maintain composure in crisis and manage their emotions to make reasoned decisions. They do not allow anger or frustration to dictate their actions but use logic and reflection to respond appropriately to challenges.
- **Focus on Virtue:** They make ethically sound decisions that benefit all stakeholders, not just those that are profitable or advantageous for themselves or their company.
- **Commitment to Justice:** Stoic leaders strive to be fair and just, ensuring their actions positively contribute to their team and community. They advocate for equality and fairness within and outside their organizational structures.

Benefits of Stoic Leadership in the Workplace

The impact of Stoic leadership extends far beyond the individual leader, influencing team dynamics, employee satisfaction, and overall organizational success. Teams led by Stoic leaders often exhibit higher levels of engagement and morale because they feel respected and valued, not just as employees but as human beings. This respect fosters a more cooperative and collaborative work environment, enhancing productivity and innovation.

Moreover, Stoic leadership contributes to a more ethical organizational culture, which can significantly reduce conflicts and moral dilemmas. When leaders handle decisions with integrity and transparency, trust is built, and ethical behavior becomes the norm rather than the exception. This ethical standard can also enhance the company's reputation, attracting like-minded employees, partners, and customers who value integrity and ethical conduct.

Research supports the efficacy of Stoic leadership practices. Studies indicate that leaders who exhibit emotional intelligence, fairness, and a focus on the collective good tend to have more resilient teams and better long-term organizational outcomes. For instance, a study examining leadership styles in multinational corporations found that leaders who practiced emotional regulation and ethical decision-making achieved higher employee retention rates and better overall performance ratings.

Interactive Element: Reflection on Your Leadership Style

Consider the following questions to reflect on your approach to leadership:

- How often do I consider the ethical implications of my decisions?
- Do I prioritize my success over the well-being of my team or organization?
- How do I respond to stress and adversity as a leader?

Reflecting on these questions can help you identify areas where you might incorporate more Stoic principles into your leadership style, enhancing your effectiveness and the well-being of your team.

In conclusion, Stoic leadership offers a model that is effective in achieving business outcomes and building a just, ethical, and supportive work environment. As you move forward in your professional journey, consider how the principles of Stoicism can guide your leadership style, helping you lead not just with authority but with virtue, integrity, and a deep commitment to the common good.

4.2 Decision-Making with Virtue: A Stoic Approach

In professional life, decision-making is often a complex landscape of competing interests, emotional pressures, and ethical dilemmas. Stoicism, emphasizing virtue and reason, provides a grounded framework for navigating these challenges. At the heart of Stoic decision-making is the belief that choices should be based not solely on outcomes or personal benefits but on whether they align with a rational and moral universe.

This approach underscores the importance of integrity, promoting decisions that contribute positively to individual success and the welfare of all involved.

Incorporating Stoic Leadership Principles

To effectively incorporate Stoic leadership principles into your own leadership style, consider the following specific strategies and techniques:

Self-Reflection: Regularly assess your actions and decisions through journaling or meditation.

Focus on Controllables: Concentrate on what you can control and accept what you cannot.

Virtue-Based Decisions: Make decisions based on wisdom, justice, courage, and temperance.

Lead by Example: Demonstrate Stoic virtues in your behavior to inspire others.

The Stoic approach to decision-making begins with a clear understanding of what is within our control and what is not. Stoics emphasize focusing efforts and choices on our actions, attitudes, and responses, recognizing that external outcomes cannot always be predicted or controlled. This perspective encourages a shift from outcome-based decision-making to virtue-based decision-making.

Ethical Decision-Making: For instance, a Stoic approach would focus on the ethical implications rather than the potential gain when faced with a business decision that could lead to significant profit but involves unethical practices. The decision to act ethically, in alignment with Stoic virtues, is considered the correct choice, regardless of the less favorable financial outcome.

Systematic Approach: A systematic approach to Stoic decision-making involves several key steps:

- Identifying what aspects of the situation are within your control.
- Considering the impact of your decision on the common good.
- Reflecting on the potential outcomes in terms of virtue.

This process begins with a thorough analysis of the situation to discern facts from assumptions, a critical step that helps focus on the elements within your sphere of influence. The decision-maker must evaluate how their potential choices align with Stoic virtues such as justice, courage, wisdom, and temperance. This evaluation considers not just the immediate effects of the decision but also its longer-term implications on one's character and others.

Real-World Applications of Stoic Decision-Making

Professionals often encounter challenges such as conflicts of interest or high-pressure situations that make Stoic decision-making difficult. For example, a manager might face pressure to cut costs by reducing staff, which could compromise product or service quality and affect employee morale. In such cases, the Stoic practice of focusing on what is virtuous promotes solutions that uphold the dignity and well-being of all parties.

The manager might instead explore alternative cost-cutting measures that do not involve layoffs, such as reducing unnecessary expenditures or improving operational efficiency. This approach addresses the immediate financial concern and maintains a commitment to justice and temperance, reinforcing a positive organizational culture.

Real-world applications of Stoic decision-making are evident in various business scenarios where ethical leadership and rational thinking have led to both successful and ethical outcomes.

Case Study: Business Ethics: Consider the case of a technology firm where the leadership faced a decision about data privacy that could affect millions of users. By applying Stoic principles, the leaders decided to enhance data protection measures, even at a significant financial cost, prioritizing their users' long-term trust and safety over short-term profits. This decision aligned with Stoic virtues and strengthened the company's reputation and customer loyalty, illustrating how virtue-based decision-making can result in sustainable success.

Case Study: Healthcare Decision-Making: Another example involves a healthcare executive deciding to invest in expensive but highly beneficial medical equipment. Despite the financial risks, the executive proceeded with the investment, guided by the Stoic principle of justice and the commitment to providing the best care possible. This decision improved patient outcomes and attracted more healthcare professionals to the institution, driven by its reputation for high-quality care and ethical management.

These examples underscore the practicality and relevance of Stoic decision-making in modern professional settings, where leaders are challenged continually to balance ethical considerations with business objectives. By adhering to Stoic principles, professionals can navigate these challenges with integrity, making decisions that advance their careers, contribute positively to society, and uphold the highest ethical standards.

As we continue to explore the intersection of Stoicism and professional life, it becomes increasingly clear that the ancient philosophy of Stoicism remains a vital guide in the complex decision-making processes of the modern world.

4.3 Handling Workplace Stress Stoically

Stress is unavoidable in the fast-paced and often high-pressure environments that characterize much of modern professional life. Yet, through the lens of Stoicism, we find a perspective that reframes stress not as an insurmountable force but as an opportunity for personal growth and resilience-building. Stoicism teaches us that stress, like all forms of adversity, is an external condition that need not disturb our internal state. This is based on the Stoic belief that our perception of events, rather than the events themselves, determines our emotional responses. Adopting a Stoic approach to stress management allows you to cultivate a mindset that views workplace challenges with clarity and composure, transforming potential stressors into opportunities for demonstrating virtue and strength.

Present Moment Focus

The Stoic technique of focusing on the present moment is pivotal in managing stress. This practice involves directing attention to your current actions and responsibilities rather than becoming overwhelmed by future uncertainties or past mistakes. For instance, during a demanding project, instead of fixating on the deadline or potential for failure, a Stoic focuses on the task at hand, channeling all energy into productive action. This mindfulness encourages a state of flow, the deep, engrossed state of involvement in the present activity, which not only reduces feelings of stress but also enhances performance and satisfaction in your work.

Control and Response

Another fundamental Stoic strategy for stress management is distinguishing between what can and cannot be controlled. This discernment is critical in reducing workplace stress, as it helps you invest your energy wisely. When faced with a challenging situation, such as an unexpected project setback, apply this Stoic distinction by asking yourself what aspects of the problem you can influence.

Perhaps you cannot change the setback, but you can control your response to it—approaching it with determination and creativity instead of frustration or resignation. This focus on actionable aspects of challenges mitigates stress and fosters a proactive and empowered approach to problem-solving.

Reflection and Learning

Reflection also plays a crucial role in Stoic stress management. Regularly reflecting on your day's work allows you to analyze your responses to stress and learn from them. Evening reflections, a staple of Stoic practice, involve:

- Review the day's events and your reactions to them.
- Identifying moments where you successfully applied Stoic principles.
- Recognizing opportunities for improvement.

This practice deepens your understanding of Stoicism and enhances your ability to use its principles in future situations, gradually increasing your resilience to stress.

Case Study: Corporate Leadership

To illustrate the effectiveness of these Stoic techniques in managing workplace stress, consider the example of a corporate team facing significant market pressures.

The team leader, a proponent of Stoicism, encouraged the team to focus only on elements within their control, such as improving product quality and customer service, rather than fixating on market fluctuations beyond their influence. This approach reduced stress within the team and led to a more creative and collaborative work environment, ultimately improving their performance and market position.

Furthermore, historical examples abound of Stoics who managed stress with remarkable composure. One poignant case is that of the philosopher Seneca, who served in the turbulent court of Emperor Nero. Despite the constant threat of political intrigue and betrayal, Senica maintained his duties with integrity and calm, using Stoic principles to navigate the perilous waters of Roman politics without succumbing to despair or cynicism. His writings from this period continue to offer guidance on facing adversity with courage and equanimity.

Incorporating Stoic practices into your daily routine can transform your approach to stress, turning workplace challenges into opportunities for demonstrating virtue and resilience. By focusing on the present, distinguishing between controllable and uncontrollable factors, and engaging in reflective practice, you can cultivate a robust inner peace that not only withstands professional pressures but thrives in spite of them.

As we conclude this exploration of Stoic strategies for managing workplace stress, remember that the goal is not to eliminate stress—an impossible and perhaps even undesirable endeavor—but to transform your relationship with stress through applying reason, virtue, and self-control. These Stoic practices equip you to face professional challenges with confidence and composure, ensuring you survive and thrive in your career. As we move forward, let these principles guide you not just in times of stress but as foundational elements of a flourishing professional life.

Reflection Questions:

1. How can Stoic principles guide your decisions and actions in a professional setting?
2. What challenges do you face in your work life that could be mitigated by Stoic practices?
3. How can you cultivate a Stoic leadership style within your workplace?

Journal Prompts:

1. Think about a difficult decision you recently made at work. Reflect on how Stoic virtues could have influenced your decision-making process.
2. Write about a time when you faced a stressful situation at work. How did you handle it, and how might a Stoic approach have altered your response?
3. Identify three areas in your professional life where you can apply Stoic principles. Develop a plan for integrating these principles into your daily work routine.

CHAPTER 5

OVERCOMING PERSONAL CHALLENGES WITH STOICISM

Striving for equilibrium in the fast-paced modern world can often feel like an uphill battle, especially as the lines between work and personal time increasingly blur. The demands of daily life, with its relentless pace and constant stream of obligations, can easily overwhelm us, leaving little room for reflection, peace, or genuine fulfillment. Yet, Stoicism, with its profound insights into life and human behavior, offers a sturdy bridge across these turbulent waters.

The Stoic philosophy, centered around living in accordance with nature and virtue, provides more than just solace in difficult times; it offers a comprehensive framework for navigating the complexities of modern life. By focusing on what is within our control and letting go of what is not, Stoicism equips us with practical strategies for managing time and priorities effectively. This approach not only helps in reducing stress but also in fostering a deeper sense of purpose and direction.

This chapter delves into how these ancient principles can be applied to modern challenges, particularly in achieving a balanced life through wise time management. It explores how Stoic practices such as reflective meditation, prioritization of tasks, and mindful living can be integrated into our daily routines to create a more harmonious and fulfilling life. By embracing these strategies, we can learn to navigate the demands of the modern world with greater ease, ultimately leading to a more balanced, purposeful, and fulfilling existence.

5.1 Achieving Work-Life Balance Through Stoic Time Management

Stoic Principles for Prioritizing Time

Stoicism teaches that living according to nature involves understanding and accepting our roles in life and the limitations imposed by external circumstances. This acceptance does not imply passivity but encourages a proactive alignment of our actions with our actual capacities and values. Time management means recognizing and embracing our roles—be they professional, familial, or personal—with a clear sense of priority that reflects our deepest values.

The Stoic concept of 'appropriate actions' (kathekon) underpins this approach to time management.

Kathekon (Appropriate Actions) Each role we undertake has its own set of appropriate actions, which are actions considered suitable to that role performed with reason and in accordance with virtue.

Example: As a parent, appropriate actions involve spending quality time with your children, supporting their education, and nurturing their growth. As a professional, it might include dedicating focused effort to your work tasks, advancing your skills, and contributing positively to your workplace environment. In the context of personal relationships, appropriate actions involve active listening, showing empathy, and being present in the moment.

These actions are not just about doing what is expected but doing it excellently and in a way that aligns with your values and virtues. By clearly defining these roles and their associated actions, you are not just managing your time, but you are taking control of your life in a way that fulfills your responsibilities and aligns with your deeper purpose and values.

This empowerment naturally fosters a balance, guiding you to invest time and energy in each area of your life, reducing conflict and the stress of over-commitment. Whether in a fast-paced corporate environment or a more relaxed academic setting, Stoic time management can be adapted to suit your needs and help you achieve a balanced life.

Practical Time Management Strategies

Effective time management, from a Stoic perspective, involves more than the mere organization of tasks—it requires a mindful presence and a focus on controlling what is within your reach. Here are some specific strategies inspired by Stoic virtues:

1. **Setting Clear Boundaries:** Just as Stoics emphasize the importance of understanding what is within our control, setting clear boundaries around your time is crucial. Determine when and how you are available for work commitments and when you reserve time for personal activities. This might mean setting specific work hours and communicating these boundaries to colleagues and family.
2. **Focusing on What is Within One's Control:** Spend your energy wisely by focusing on tasks and responsibilities you can directly influence. Avoid worrying about outcomes beyond your control, which derails productivity and increases stress.

3. **Practicing Presence:** Engage fully with the task at hand, whether it's a work project or time spent with family. This practice not only improves the quality of your work and relationships but also helps to prevent the mental strain of multitasking, which can dilute your effectiveness and satisfaction.

Case Studies of Successful Stoic Time Management

Consider the story of a corporate executive overwhelmed by the demands of her high-stakes job and her responsibilities as a mother. By applying Stoic principles, she began to categorize her daily activities into those that were essential and aligned with her values and those that were not. She started delegating non-essential tasks at work and set specific times for uninterrupted family activities. This improved her productivity at work and enhanced her relationships at home, creating a more fulfilling balance in her life.

Similarly, a student could use Stoic time management to balance academic responsibilities with personal growth, or a retiree could apply these principles to balance leisure activities with community service. A teenager could use Stoic time management to balance school, extracurricular activities, and personal time. In contrast a young professional could use it to balance career growth, personal relationships, and self-care.

Another example is a small business owner who used Stoic exercises to prioritize his time after feeling burnt out from constant work. He implemented a daily practice of reflecting on his key roles and the appropriate actions required for each. This reflection helped him realize that he was neglecting his health, a crucial aspect of his ability to perform other roles effectively. He adjusted his schedule to include regular exercise and meditation, significantly improving his well-being and business performance.

Arnold Schwarzenegger, the iconic bodybuilder, actor, and politician, has often spoken about how Stoic principles have influenced his approach to time management and success. By integrating Stoicism into his daily routine, Schwarzenegger has achieved remarkable feats across multiple fields.

Tools and Exercises for Implementation

To integrate these Stoic strategies into your daily life, consider the following tools and exercises:

Create a Virtue-Based Schedule: Design your daily or weekly schedule around Stoic virtues. Assign time blocks based on tasks and the virtues you want to cultivate. For instance, allocate time for activities that enhance wisdom (like reading or learning), courage (such as tackling challenging tasks), justice (time spent helping others), and temperance (activities that promote self-control and moderation). Additionally, you can use Stoic journaling to reflect on your day and identify areas where you can improve your time management or practice Stoic mindfulness to stay present and focused on your tasks.

Conduct a Weekly Review of Time Spent Versus Value Gained: At the end of each week, review how you spent your time and assess this against the value gained regarding personal growth, fulfillment, and contributions to your roles. This review helps you see where to be more accurate with your time and reinforces your commitment to living by Stoic principles.

Through these practices, Stoicism offers a theoretical guide to living well and practical tools that address one of the most pressing challenges of modern life: managing our time to fulfill our responsibilities while allowing for personal growth and well-being. Adopting a Stoic approach to time management empowers you to live a more balanced and productive life and brings a deep sense of fulfillment, knowing that you are following your values and priorities.

5.2 Coping with Personal Loss: A Stoic Perspective

Understanding Loss and Impermanence

The Stoic philosophy, with its deep roots in the awareness of nature's cycles, offers a profound understanding of loss and impermanence. According to Stoicism, everything in the universe constantly changes, where beginnings are invariably tied to ends, and creation is linked with dissolution. This worldview holds that human life, too, adheres to this natural order of birth, existence, and cessation. By understanding and accepting this cycle, Stoicism equips you with the philosophical tools to face loss—not just as an inevitable part of life but as an integral component of the universe's rhythm.

When you internalize the Stoic view of impermanence, the pain associated with personal loss shifts; it doesn't vanish or diminish the value or significance of what has been lost. Instead, this perspective helps mitigate the sharpness of grief by framing loss within the broader context of life's transient nature. Recognizing that every life, relationship, and material possession has its season, you can begin to view loss through a lens of gratitude for the time and experiences shared rather than solely through a lens of sorrow for what is no longer present.

Cultivating Emotional Resilience

In cultivating emotional resilience in the face of loss, Stoicism emphasizes accepting what cannot be changed. This acceptance is grounded in the Stoics' distinction between what is within our control and what is not. Grieving, a natural and healthy response to loss, is viewed under Stoicism as a part of the human experience that we can approach with sensitivity and rationality. You are encouraged to allow yourself to experience and express grief fully, yet Stoic wisdom teaches you to do so without letting it define or overwhelm you. This approach fosters inner resilience, enabling you to navigate through grief with composure and emerge with a renewed sense of purpose.

Guidance from Stoic Philosophers

The writings of Stoic philosophers are rich with guidance and consolation on dealing with loss. In his letters, Seneca offers profound insights into the nature of grief and consolation. He suggests that while we cannot control loss, we can control our response to it, advocating for a stance of courage and dignity in the face of sorrow. His words provide not just comfort but a framework for processing and integrating loss into the fabric of life, encouraging a reflective rather than reactive response to grief.

Personal Stories of Stoic Coping

Historical and contemporary figures alike have drawn on Stoic principles to manage personal loss with grace and stability. One poignant example is Admiral James Stockdale, who relied on his understanding of Epictetus's teachings to endure years of captivity during the Vietnam War. Stockdale's situation, though extreme, underscores the power of Stoic philosophy in facing loss—of freedom, in his case—with resilience. He credits Stoicism for helping him accept his circumstances without bitterness, focusing instead on maintaining his integrity and leading his fellow prisoners with strength and compassion.

In a more relatable context, consider the story of a modern professional who turned to Stoicism after the sudden loss of a spouse. Through daily engagement with Stoic texts and practices, this individual found a framework to process their grief that emphasized personal agency and accepting life's impermanence. They practiced Stoic reflections, focusing on cherishing the memories of shared experiences while acknowledging that the future must be met with a renewed sense of purpose and engagement in life.

These stories, and countless others like them, illustrate how Stoicism does not numb us to pain or strip away the emotional realities of loss. Instead, it offers a way to incorporate loss into our lives in a manner that honors both our vulnerability and our strength. By embracing Stoic principles, you equip yourself with philosophical tools that help transform the loss experience from a narrative of despair to one of understanding, acceptance, and eventual peace.

Transforming Loss into Growth

In engaging with these Stoic practices and perspectives, dealing with loss becomes a path to deeper self-understanding and an enhanced appreciation for the transient beauty of life. Stoicism teaches that in our response to loss, we can find profound opportunities for growth and reaffirmation of our values, allowing us to continue forward with a poised heart and a clear mind. As you incorporate these teachings into your life, remember that the Stoic approach to loss is not about diminishing the pain but weaving it into the larger tapestry of your life's journey, marked by an enduring pursuit of wisdom and virtue.

5.3 Stoic Wisdom on Managing Relationship Conflicts

Conflicts are inevitable in the intricate dance of human relationships. Yet, if approached with the wisdom and principles of Stoicism, they need not lead to lasting discord or resentment. With its rich insights into human behavior and emotion, Stoicism offers valuable guidance on nurturing relationships through understanding, empathy, and rationality. It teaches us to view conflicts not merely as hurdles but as opportunities for personal growth and strengthening bonds through virtue.

Perceptions and Reactions

Stoic philosophy posits that the quality of our relationships hinges significantly on our perceptions and reactions. By adopting a Stoic mindset, we learn to focus on our contributions to conflicts and control our responses rather than attempting to control the behavior of others.

This approach begins with a deep commitment to understanding and empathy.

Understanding and Empathy

Stoicism encourages us to consider the perspectives of others not as opposing but as opportunities to expand our understanding. For example, amid a disagreement, a Stoic-inspired response involves actively listening to the other person's viewpoint and striving to comprehend their reasoning and emotions. This does not imply agreement but acknowledges the complexity of human perspectives and the value of diverse experiences.

Empathy in Stoic practice extends beyond mere emotional resonance; it involves rationalizing why individuals might feel or behave in specific ways. This understanding is crucial in de-escalating conflicts and fostering a supportive dialogue. It allows for a communication style that is clear, honest, and, most importantly, non-confrontational. Stoics advocate for discussions free of harsh criticism or defensiveness but guided instead by a genuine quest for mutual understanding and resolution.

Emotional Detachment

Maintaining emotional detachment plays a vital role in Stoic conflict resolution. This does not mean suppressing or ignoring emotions but refraining from allowing them to cloud judgment or escalate the conflict. It involves acknowledging one's feelings, understanding their origins, and choosing a response based on reason and virtue rather than impulse. For instance, if a colleague's remark stirs anger, a Stoic approach would involve taking a moment to ponder why the remark was upsetting, considering any underlying issues that might need addressing, and then responding in a manner that aims to clarify and resolve rather than retaliate.

Stoic Virtues in Relationships

Stoic virtues—patience, justice, and temperance—are indispensable in sustaining healthy relationships.

- **Patience** allows us to give others the time and space to express themselves without rushing to judgment.
- **Justice** involves treating others fairly and respectfully, even in disagreement, ensuring that our actions and words do not cause undue harm.
- **Temperance**, or self-control, helps moderate our responses, ensuring they are proportionate and appropriate to the situation.

Historical and Modern Examples

These Stoic strategies have proven effective in managing relationship conflicts in historical and contemporary contexts. Consider the example of a historical Stoic figure like Cato the Younger, known for his steadfast adherence to Stoic virtues amidst the political intrigue of ancient Rome. Even with his adversaries, Cato's interactions were marked by a firm yet fair approach that sought resolution through principled dialogue, not power plays.

In a modern setting, imagine a family where tensions over differing life choices and values could easily brew into conflicts. Through Stoic practices, family members can learn to respectfully express their views and seek common ground, acknowledging individual differences while reinforcing their bonds.

Transforming Interactions

These principles are theoretical ideals and practical tools that can transform everyday interactions into more meaningful and supportive encounters. As you navigate the complexities of your relationships, incorporating Stoic wisdom can help you manage conflicts with clarity and composure, turning potential discord into opportunities for deeper understanding and connection.

Moving forward, remember that the essence of Stoic conflict management lies not in avoiding disagreement but in engaging with it constructively. By practicing Stoic virtues, focusing on effective communication, and maintaining a commitment to understanding and empathy, you can build and sustain relationships that are not only resilient in the face of conflicts but are also enriched by them. This Stoic approach to relationships offers a path to personal growth and harmony, guided by the timeless wisdom of this profound philosophical tradition.

As we conclude this exploration of Stoic wisdom on managing relationship conflicts, we see how the ancient principles of Stoicism remain profoundly relevant in our modern lives. They offer guidance that helps us navigate the complexities of human relationships with grace and virtue. This journey through Stoic thought is not merely about learning philosophical concepts but integrating them into our daily interactions, transforming potential conflicts into opportunities for growth and deeper connection.

In the next chapter, we will delve into how Stoicism can provide insights into achieving personal fulfillment and happiness, further exploring the practical applications of this enriching philosophical tradition in our everyday lives.

Reflection Questions:

1. How can Stoic philosophy help you navigate personal losses or setbacks?
2. In what ways does Stoicism encourage resilience in the face of adversity?
3. How can you apply the Stoic virtues to manage conflicts in your personal relationships?

Journal Prompts:

1. Reflect on a personal loss you have experienced. How can Stoic principles help you find peace and understanding in this situation?
2. Write about a conflict you are currently facing. How can you approach this conflict with a Stoic mindset to achieve a resolution?
3. Describe a recent challenge you faced. How did you respond, and how might applying Stoic virtues change your approach in the future?

CHAPTER 6

STOICISM AND COMMUNITY ENGAGEMENT

In the intricate web of modern society, where individual actions can ripple out to affect a global community, the Stoic philosophy provides a profound framework for understanding our roles as individuals and as integral members of a larger collective. Stoicism teaches us that each person is a citizen of the world, a concept encapsulated in the idea of the 'cosmopolis.' This notion transcends local affiliations, national boundaries, and parochial interests, urging us to embrace our duties to humanity. In this chapter, we explore the profound impact of Stoic philosophy on community engagement, emphasizing the duties and responsibilities it entails and the role of virtue in public life.

6.1 The Stoic as a Citizen: Duties and Responsibilities

Defining the Stoic Citizen

Stoicism introduces us to the concept of 'cosmopolis,' or world citizenship, where every individual is considered part of a universal polity connected by reason and shared virtues. This revolutionary perspective expands our sense of community beyond immediate geographical or cultural boundaries to include the entire human race. As citizens of the world, Stoics advocate for a life led by principles that uphold the common good, transcending personal or local interests. This global outlook does not negate one's regional or national identities but rather places them within a broader context of universal human dignity and interconnectedness.

Duties toward Community and Society

As a Stoic, your duties to the community are not limited to passive coexistence but involve active participation and contribution to the common welfare. These duties are founded on Stoic ethical principles, particularly justice and benevolence. Acting with justice in this context means treating every individual fairly and impartially, ensuring that your actions contribute positively to the welfare of others. Engaging in public service, whether through volunteering, participating in governance, or simply helping a neighbor, is a practical expression of this commitment. Promoting common welfare also involves advocating for policies and practices that benefit society, particularly the most vulnerable members.

A Stoic's approach to community duties is proactive and grounded in the practice of virtue. For example, consider the environmental challenges facing our planet. A Stoic recognizes a duty to engage in sustainable practices, not just for personal benefit or compliance with social trends, but as a fundamental responsibility to the global community and future generations. This might involve making choices that reduce one's ecological footprint, supporting policies that protect the environment, or educating others about sustainable practices.

Role of Virtue in Public Life

The practice of Stoic virtues—wisdom, courage, justice, and temperance—is crucial in fulfilling one's duties as a citizen. These virtues not only guide personal conduct but also one's engagement in public life. Wisdom involves making informed, ethical decisions that reflect an understanding of the complex interdependencies within a community. Courage enables individuals to stand up for their principles, speak out against injustice, and take actions that may be unpopular but are proper and necessary. This empowerment through virtue is a key aspect of Stoic philosophy.

Specific Examples of Stoic Virtues Applied to Public Life Justice

Example: Marcus Aurelius, a Roman Emperor and a prominent Stoic philosopher, applied the virtue of justice by governing with fairness and a commitment to the well-being of his people. He emphasized the importance of serving the common good and making decisions that were beneficial to the majority.

Wisdom

Example: Epictetus, a former enslaved person turned Stoic philosopher, exemplified wisdom through his teachings on understanding what is within our control and what is not. He used his deep understanding of human nature and Stoic principles to guide others in making rational decisions and living a life aligned with virtue, regardless of external circumstances. His emphasis on inner freedom and rationality continues to inspire those seeking wisdom in the face of life's challenges.

Courage

Example: Nelson Mandela, though not a Stoic by philosophy, embodied the Stoic virtue of courage during his fight against apartheid in South Africa. He faced immense personal risk and hardship while standing firm in his principles and working towards justice and equality.

Temperance

Example: Frederick Douglass, the influential abolitionist and former enslaved person, exhibited temperance in his advocacy by practicing self-discipline and moderation, particularly in his pursuit of justice through peaceful means and reasoned discourse, rather than resorting to violence, setting a moral standard for future civil rights leaders.

Temperance, or self-control, ensures one's desires or ambitions are consistent with the community's more significant needs. It fosters a balanced approach to public engagement, where rational deliberation rather than impulsive reactions guide actions. For instance, a Stoic would strive to respond thoughtfully and respectfully in a heated public debate, focusing on the argument's merits rather than the heat of emotions.

Case Studies of Stoic Citizenship

Historical and contemporary examples abound of individuals who have exemplified Stoic citizenship. One notable figure is Cato the Younger, a Roman statesman known for his unwavering commitment to the Roman Republic's ideals. Despite personal risk, he consistently placed the state's welfare above his own, challenging corruption and advocating for governance reforms. Though marked by political turmoil, his life is a testament to the impact of Stoic virtues in public service.

In more recent times, consider the efforts of individuals like Malala Yousafzai, who, though not explicitly a Stoic, embodies Stoic virtues through her advocacy for girls' education. Her courageous stand against oppressive forces, driven by a profound sense of justice and a commitment to the common good, resonates deeply with Stoic principles. Her actions have advanced educational opportunities for girls and inspired a global movement toward greater equality and justice.

These examples underscore the transformative potential of living as a Stoic citizen. By embracing our duties to the broader community and grounding our actions in virtue, we contribute to a more just, compassionate, and rational world. As you reflect on your role within this global community, consider how practicing Stoic virtues can enhance your effectiveness and integrity as a citizen, not just in your local context but as part of the interconnected human polity. This approach to community engagement, guided by Stoic principles, offers a pathway to meaningful change and a deeper connection with the world around us.

As we continue to explore the rich tapestry of Stoic philosophy and its application to modern life, let us carry forward the spirit of global citizenship, motivated by a commitment to virtue and the common good. In doing so, we enrich our lives and contribute to the flourishing of our communities and the world at large.

6.2 Stoicism and Social Justice: Advocating with Temperance

In the vast social justice arena, where passions run high, and the stakes are significant, Stoicism offers a grounding perspective that fuels the pursuit of equality and justice and ensures sustainability in advocacy efforts. Stoicism compels us to seek justice, rooted in the principle that all human beings are inherently equal and deserving of dignity and respect. This philosophical stance drives us to challenge injustices not as external warriors but as individuals embodying the virtues of wisdom, courage, justice, and temperance. Here, temperance plays a critical role, particularly in advocacy, as it tempers passion with reason, ensuring our efforts are effective and enduring.

The Role of Cosmopolis in Social Justice

The Stoic pursuit of justice is deeply connected to the 'cosmopolis,' or the idea of a global community where every individual, regardless of background, is considered part of a collective humanity. This view compels us to advocate for policies and practices that uphold the universal values of fairness and dignity. However, balancing our zeal with Stoic temperance is crucial in the heat of advocacy.

This virtue is not about diminishing passion but about channeling it wisely. It involves self-control and moderation, essential in preventing burnout—a common risk for many passionate advocates. By practicing temperance, you ensure that your advocacy is not a fleeting outburst of passion but a sustained effort guided by rational thought and a deep commitment to justice.

Practical Stoic Strategies for Advocates

Stoic strategies for advocates emphasize focusing on what is within one's control. In the context of social justice, this means directing your efforts towards actions that can make a difference, such as educating oneself and others, participating in peaceful demonstrations, or engaging in community organizing. It also involves using reasoned dialogue to influence public opinion and policy making. Stoicism teaches us to engage in conversations that are not about winning arguments but about seeking truth and understanding. This approach fosters a more inclusive and constructive public discourse, where diverse perspectives are heard and valued, and solutions are sought in the spirit of mutual respect and cooperation.

Historical Examples of Stoic-Inspired Advocacy

A powerful illustration of Stoic-inspired advocacy can be seen in the civil rights movement in the United States. Figures like Martin Luther King Jr., although not explicitly a Stoic, embodied Stoic virtues in his approach to civil rights advocacy. Mr King emphasized nonviolent resistance and appealed to universal human rights and dignity, reflecting Stoic principles of justice and temperance. His ability to channel passionate advocacy into organized, thoughtful action has left a lasting impact, demonstrating the effectiveness of Stoic strategies in achieving profound social change.

Contemporary Examples of Stoic Principles in Advocacy

Recently, the global environmental movement has also showcased Stoic principles in action. Advocates for climate justice focus on what is within their control—raising awareness, reducing personal carbon footprints, and pushing for policy changes—while maintaining a composed and rational approach in the face of daunting challenges. This movement, driven by urgency and temperance, highlights how Stoic virtues can inform and sustain modern advocacy efforts, leading to meaningful and lasting change.

By embracing Stoic principles in your advocacy efforts, you contribute to pursuing justice and ensure that your actions are guided by reason and virtue. This approach enhances the effectiveness of your advocacy and aligns your efforts with a broader philosophical tradition that values dignity, equality, and the common good. As you continue to advocate for social justice, let Stoicism remind you that actual change is a product of persistent, reasoned, and virtuous effort—a commitment to transforming the world for the moment and future generations.

6.3 Building Resilient Communities through Stoic Practices

In contemplating the fabric of resilient communities, one finds that their strength often emanates from economic resources or infrastructural robustness and the depth of their communal bonds and collective ethos. With its rich teachings on virtue, self-discipline, and mutual support, Stoicism provides insightful principles that can significantly fortify community resilience. This resilience manifests through enhanced mutual support, shared strength, and a collective repository of wisdom, enabling communities to withstand adversities and thrive amidst them.

Community resilience in Stoicism extends beyond the survival of crises; it involves a transformation wherein community members grow closer, learn, and emerge stronger. This growth is cultivated through the

Stoic emphasis on supporting one another in practicing virtue and facing challenges with a unified front. For instance, communal reflections—a practice where community members gather to discuss philosophical and ethical aspects of life—can reinforce communal bonds.

These reflections allow individuals to share personal experiences and insights, fostering a deeper understanding and empathy among community members. Such practices strengthen emotional bonds and create a shared purpose and commitment to the common good. Shared meditations also play a crucial role in enhancing community resilience. These sessions involve community members meditating on Stoic teachings, such as the impermanence of external conditions and the importance of inner tranquility.

By focusing collectively on these principles, communities can cultivate a shared psychological resilience, enabling them to maintain a calm and composed demeanor in the face of external tumults. This shared sense of calm significantly contributes to the overall stability and resilience of the community, as individuals feel psychologically supported and less isolated in their struggles.

Stoic leaders—individuals who embody Stoic virtues and lead by example—are critical in nurturing community resilience. Such leaders inspire resilience by demonstrating how to face challenges with courage and equanimity, encouraging community members to adopt similar attitudes. During times of crisis, be it natural disasters, economic downturns, or social upheavals, Stoic leaders can steer the community through turmoil by making decisions that reflect practical wisdom and moral integrity. They prioritize the welfare of all community members, ensuring that actions taken during crises do not benefit a select few but are aimed at the greater good of the entire community.

Case Studies of Stoic Communities

In May 2007, the small town of Greensburg, Kansas, was almost entirely destroyed by an EF5 tornado, one of the most powerful tornadoes recorded in U.S. history. The tornado left 95% of the town in ruins, devastating homes, businesses, and infrastructure. Faced with overwhelming destruction, the residents of Greensburg were confronted with a choice: to rebuild their town or to abandon it. The decision they made exemplifies resilience, collective action, and forward-thinking, closely mirroring Stoic principles in action.

Rather than succumbing to despair, the people of Greensburg chose to see the disaster as an opportunity to rebuild in a way that would not only restore what was lost but also create a more sustainable and resilient community. They adopted a vision of making Greensburg a model of green living, focusing on sustainability and energy efficiency. This decision reflects the Stoic principle of focusing on what is within one's control. While they could not change the fact that the tornado had destroyed their town, they could control how they responded to the disaster and how they rebuilt.

The rebuilding process in Greensburg was marked by a strong sense of community and collective action. Residents, local leaders, and outside experts came together to plan and execute a reconstruction that would benefit everyone. They held town meetings and discussions where every voice could be heard, ensuring that the rebuilding process was inclusive and that the entire community was invested in the future of the town. This collaborative effort embodies the Stoic value of mutual support and the importance of working together towards the common good.

One of the key outcomes of Greensburg's rebuilding effort was the decision to incorporate green technologies and sustainable practices throughout the town. This included building energy-efficient homes, using renewable energy sources, and constructing public buildings to the highest environmental standards. The town even adopted the motto *"Greensburg: Better, Stronger, Greener,"* reflecting their commitment to not just recovering from the disaster, but using it as a springboard to create a more sustainable future. This forward-thinking approach is reminiscent of Stoic wisdom, where adversity is transformed into an opportunity for growth and improvement.

Today, Greensburg stands as a testament to the power of resilience and community spirit. The town's decision to rebuild in a sustainable way has garnered attention and praise from around the world, serving as an example of how communities can turn disaster into an opportunity for positive change. The story of Greensburg, Kansas, is a powerful reminder that even in the face of overwhelming adversity, it is possible to focus on what is within our control, work together as a community, and emerge stronger and more resilient.

Reflection Questions:

1. How can Stoic philosophy guide your contributions to your community?
2. What are the key responsibilities of a Stoic citizen, and how can you fulfill these roles?
3. How can you advocate for social justice while maintaining Stoic temperance and rationality?

Journal Prompts:

1. Reflect on your role within your community. How can you embody Stoic virtues to make a positive impact?
2. Write about a social issue you are passionate about. How can you approach this issue using Stoic principles to advocate effectively and sustainably?

Identify a community project or initiative you would like to get involved in. Develop a plan for how you will contribute to this cause while practicing Stoic virtues.

Make a Difference with Your Review

Unlock the Power of Generosity

"Do not forget that you are a part of a greater whole; what benefits others benefits you. Helping others is not only a duty, but it is also a path to finding your own peace and fulfillment."

Inspired by Marcus Aurelius

Helping others makes you feel good and can even lead to a longer, happier life. So, let's try to make a difference together!

Here's a question for you...

Would you help someone you've never met, even if you never got credit for it?

This person is just like you used to be. They want to embrace Stoic principles, need some guidance, and are not sure where to look. My mission is to make Stoic Philosophy accessible to everyone. Everything I do stems from that mission. And the only way for me to accomplish that mission is by reaching. . .well...everyone.

This is where you come in. Most people judge a book by its cover (and its reviews). So here's my ask on behalf of a struggling author you've never met:

Please help that future Stoic by leaving this book a review.

Your gift costs no money and less than 60 seconds to make, but can change a fellow seeker's life forever. Your review could help. . .

...one more person discover the power of resilience.

...one more individual find peace amidst chaos.

...one more reader cultivate inner strength.

...one more soul embark on a path of wisdom.

...one more dream of living virtuously come true.

To get that 'feel good' feeling and help this person for real, all you have to do is...and it takes less than 60 seconds... leave a review.

Simply scan the QR code or follow the link below to leave your review:

https://mybook.to/StoicPhilosophy

If you feel good about helping a faceless Stoic, you are my kind of person. Welcome to the club. You're one of us.

I'm that much more excited to help you explore Stoic philosophy by providing practical insights and timeless wisdom faster than you can possibly imagine. You'll love the reflections I'm about to share in the coming chapters.

Thank you from the bottom of my heart. Now, back to our regularly scheduled programming.

Your biggest fan,

Alex

CHAPTER 7

HISTORICAL INSIGHTS AND MODERN APPLICATIONS

As the sun rises anew each day, the enduring relevance of Stoicism continues to illuminate paths through the complexities of modern life. This ancient philosophy, crafted amid the tumult and triumphs of early civilization, has survived the relentless march of time and thrived, evolving and adapting to meet the needs of successive generations. In this chapter, we delve into the profound journey of Stoicism, from the reflective writings of Marcus Aurelius to its significant resurgence in contemporary society. Through this exploration, you will discover how Stoic principles have been seamlessly woven into modern psychological practices, leadership theories, and educational systems, offering timeless solutions to today's challenges.

7.1 From Marcus Aurelius to Modern Day: Stoic Evolution

Overview of Marcus Aurelius' Contributions to Stoicism

Marcus Aurelius, often called 'the philosopher king,' remains one of the most respected figures in Stoic history, not merely for his role as a Roman emperor but for his profound contributions to Stoic philosophy. His seminal work, *Meditations*, penned as a series of personal writings and reflections, offers a window into his inner life and the application of Stoicism to his duties and responsibilities. Aurelius's writings encapsulate the essence of Stoic philosophy—his relentless pursuit of self-improvement, his unwavering commitment to ruling with justice and temperance, and his profound understanding of the impermanence of human existence.

In *Meditations*, Aurelius emphasizes the importance of self-control, accepting fate, and acting according to reason, irrespective of personal emotions. These themes resonate as philosophical ideals and practical approaches to life's challenges. His thoughts on facing adversity, maintaining integrity in the face of temptation, and finding tranquility amidst chaos have guided countless individuals in seeking a life of virtue and meaning.

Evolution of Stoic Thought Post-Aurelius

The trajectory of Stoic philosophy did not culminate with Marcus Aurelius but instead sparked a legacy that would permeate through the ages. Stoicism faced a period of decline after the fall of the Roman Empire; however, its core ideals survived and found new expressions in various philosophical and religious movements throughout the Middle Ages and the Renaissance. During these times, Stoic virtues were often harmonized with Christian teachings, emphasizing ethics and personal integrity.

The Renaissance revived interest in classical philosophies, including Stoicism, which influenced the era's art, science, and humanistic studies. Thinkers like Justus Lipsius carried Stoic ideals forward, advocating for reason and natural law. This period marked a significant chapter in the evolution of Stoicism, as it was revisited through various philosophical lenses, contributing to Enlightenment thinking and contemporary existential and virtue ethics.

Revival in the 20th and 21st Centuries

Stoicism's remarkable resurgence in the 20th and 21st centuries can be attributed to its practical relevance to contemporary issues such as stress management, personal development, and leadership. Figures like Viktor Frankl, who survived the Holocaust, and James Stockdale, a United States Navy vice admiral, drew heavily on Stoic principles. Their experiences underscored Stoicism's utility in facing extreme adversity with courage and resilience, demonstrating its enduring relevance in the face of modern challenges.

Today, Stoicism influences various spheres, including psychology, where its principles underpin Cognitive Behavioral Therapy (CBT), a therapeutic approach that helps individuals reframe their thinking and manage emotional responses effectively. In leadership, Stoic virtues guide leaders in managing their responsibilities with integrity and foresight, fostering environments based on respect and rationality.

Contemporary Applications and Adaptations

The adaptability of Stoic principles is vividly illustrated in their application across diverse modern contexts. In educational curriculums, for instance, Stoicism is incorporated into courses that explore ethics, leadership, and personal development. In the corporate world,

Stoic practices enhance leadership training programs, emphasizing emotional intelligence, ethical decision-making, and stress management. These programs draw on Stoic ideas to cultivate influential leaders who achieve organizational goals and wise, just, and compassionate leaders who empower individuals with practical tools for success.

These programs utilize Stoic principles to develop leaders who effectively reach organizational objectives and are wise, fair, and empathetic.

Furthermore, Stoicism has found a place in popular culture, influencing books, blogs, and seminars that teach resilience and the pursuit of a meaningful life. Its principles are often adapted into practical exercises that individuals can incorporate into their daily routines, helping them to meet personal and professional challenges with grace and virtue. This widespread influence of Stoicism in popular culture is a testament to its enduring relevance and practicality.

Stoicism's journey from ancient philosophy to a vital component of modern life underscores its enduring relevance. It offers a beacon of stability and wisdom that continues to guide us through the complexities of contemporary existence, providing tools for resilience, ethical living, and personal fulfillment. As we continue to navigate the challenges of our times, the lessons of Stoicism remain as applicable today as they were in the days of Marcus Aurelius, connecting us to timeless wisdom.

7.2 Stoic Responses to Global Crises: Past and Present

In times of profound crisis, the principles of Stoicism have historically provided guidance and comfort to leaders and communities, offering practical strategies for enduring and overcoming great adversities. The resilience and clarity of Stoicism are particularly evident during some of the most challenging periods in history.

Case Study: Marcus Aurelius and the Antonine Plague

A notable example is during the reign of Marcus Aurelius, when the Antonine Plague struck the Roman Empire. This devastating epidemic weakened the Roman army, debilitated the population, and required extraordinary leadership and resolve. Marcus Aurelius, a Stoic philosopher, faced this crisis with a steadfast commitment to duty and the common good. His responses were not merely reactive; they were deeply rooted in the Stoic belief that one must accept events beyond one's control while actively addressing what can be influenced. Aurelius's handling of the plague included measures to support the Roman people, such as providing financial aid to the afflicted and maintaining essential public services.

Leadership Rooted in Stoic Principles

Despite personal losses and immense pressure, Marcus Aurelius's leadership exemplified Stoic principles: maintaining composure, focusing on practical solutions, and prioritizing the welfare of his people over personal grief. Stoic crisis management is grounded in three core tenets: virtue, the common good, and acceptance of events beyond one's control. These principles foster psychological resilience, enabling individuals and leaders to navigate crises by focusing on actionable steps rather than succumbing to despair over uncontrollable circumstances.

The Stoic Perspective on Crisis as Opportunity

Stoicism teaches that every crisis, while undeniably challenging, also presents opportunities for growth and the reaffirmation of communal bonds. It encourages a perspective that looks beyond the immediate impact of the crisis to the long-term well-being of the community.

Modern Application: The Global Response to COVID-19

The COVID-19 pandemic, for example, had a significant global impact, affecting all aspects of life, including health, the economy, and daily routines. The pandemic tested the resilience of nations, healthcare systems, and communities worldwide. Governments and healthcare organizations were challenged to respond effectively, while individuals had to adapt to new measures such as social distancing and mask-wearing. The pandemic highlighted the importance of global cooperation and collective responsibility in combating a shared threat. It also spurred innovations in healthcare, technology, and remote work, and accelerated the development of vaccines and treatments.

Collective Resilience Inspired by Stoicism

The global response to the COVID-19 pandemic demonstrated the strength and adaptability of human societies in the face of unprecedented challenges. Similarly, communities that embrace Stoic teachings often recover more cohesively from natural disasters such as hurricanes and earthquakes. Stoicism inspires collective resilience by focusing on community support, equitable distribution of resources, and a composed reassessment of rebuilding strategies. Accepting the impact of the event is balanced with a proactive commitment to recovery and future preparedness, embodying the Stoic resolve to endure and rebuild.

Lessons for the Future: Stoic Strategies in Crisis Management

Looking to the future, the lessons drawn from Stoic philosophy are invaluable in shaping crisis management strategies. Preparation, a key Stoic strategy, involves not only physical readiness, such as infrastructure development and resource management, but also psychological preparedness, where communities are fortified with the mental resilience to face potential crises. Fostering a perspective that emphasizes the common good can guide policy decisions, ensuring that actions taken during crises do not merely serve immediate needs but also contribute to long-term stability and improvement.

The Role of Ethical Leadership in Crisis

Moreover, the importance of ethical leadership in crises cannot be overstated. Leaders who embody Stoic virtues—those who demonstrate rationality, integrity, and a deep concern for those they lead—are instrumental in navigating crises successfully. Their ability to maintain a clear-headed approach, even under severe pressure, is a stabilizing force, encouraging rational and calm responses from others.

Stoicism's Relevance in Contemporary Global Challenges

As we continue to face global challenges, from climate change to geopolitical conflicts, the Stoic principles of thoughtful resilience, community focus, and virtuous leadership remain as relevant as ever. These principles not only help us manage crises when they arise but also strengthen the social fabric, ensuring that communities are not just prepared to survive but are also equipped to thrive in the face of adversity. Therefore, Stoicism's enduring wisdom is not just historical but a continuing legacy that offers profound insights into managing the complexities of modern-day crises.

7.3 The Stoic Influence on Western Thought

The tendrils of Stoic philosophy have woven through the fabric of Western thought, subtly but significantly shaping its development over centuries. Stoicism, with its robust framework of virtue and rationality, has left an indelible mark on various intellectual and cultural domains, from early Christian teachings to the rigorous discourses of the Enlightenment and into the nuanced dialogues of modern philosophical movements. The adaptability and enduring relevance of Stoic ideas underscore their profound utility in addressing the ethical and existential questions that have perennially confronted humanity.

Impact on Early Christian Thought

The early Christian thinkers found a resonant voice in Stoicism that echoed their emphasis on virtues and ethical living. The integration of Stoic moral ethics into Christian doctrine during the formative years of Christianity was not merely coincidental but a deliberate synthesis aimed at enriching Christian ethical practices. Stoic concepts such as the natural law, universal brotherhood, and cultivating virtues like temperance and fortitude were harmoniously woven into Christian teachings, enhancing Christian doctrine's moral and philosophical depth.

For example, the Stoic concept of logos, the rational principle that governs the universe, influenced Christian theology's concept of the Word (Logos) as articulated in the Gospel of John. This Stoic influence extended to the emphasis on living a life of virtue in accordance with divine reason, a principle that deeply informed Christian ascetic practices and the moral teachings of the Church Fathers. The convergence of Stoic and Christian thought enriched the spiritual and ethical landscape of early Christianity, providing followers with a more comprehensive framework for understanding virtue, suffering, and the human condition.

Stoicism and the Enlightenment

As the light of reason began to spread across Europe during the Enlightenment, Stoic philosophy experienced a revival as thinkers sought to ground the burgeoning ideals of liberty, equality, and fraternity in a solid philosophical foundation. The Enlightenment philosophers, notably Immanuel Kant, found a compelling model of rationality and ethical rigor in Stoicism. Kant's categorical imperative commands individuals to act only according to maxims that can be universalized. This mirrors the Stoic emphasis on universal reason and the obligation to act virtuously irrespective of personal desires or circumstances.

The Stoic virtues, particularly the commitment to rational public discourse and civic duty, resonated with Enlightenment values and influenced debates surrounding governance, justice, and human rights. The Stoic ideal of a cosmopolitan society, in which all individuals are citizens of the world and bound by common rationality, bolstered the Enlightenment's vision of a globally interconnected human community governed by reason and mutual respect.

Influence on Modern Philosophical Movements

Stoicism continues to echo in the contemporary philosophical landscape, notably in existentialism and pragmatism. The focus on individual responsibility and the practical application of philosophy in everyday life reveal clear parallels with Stoic thought. Existentialists, though often centered on the individual's confrontation with meaninglessness, share with Stoics the idea that individuals possess the freedom to craft their own lives through choices aligned with personal integrity and authenticity.

Pragmatism, emphasizing the practical consequences of beliefs and actions, similarly resonates with Stoic ideas. Stoicism promotes a precise evaluation of life's challenges and a pragmatic approach to solving them through virtue and reason, a method pragmatists may appreciate.

Stoicism in Contemporary Cultural and Educational Contexts

Today, Stoicism permeates various aspects of modern culture, proving its relevance and adaptability. In educational settings, Stoicism enriches philosophy, psychology, and even business studies syllabi, where its principles underpin lessons on ethical leadership, resilience, and decision-making. In popular media, Stoicism has been featured in books, podcasts, and online platforms, often focused on personal development and self-help, reflecting the growing public interest in its practical benefits.

Moreover, Stoic principles have been effectively integrated into professional training programs, particularly those focusing on stress management and leadership. These programs use Stoic emotional regulation techniques and rational problem-solving to foster productive, wise, and just professional environments.

Stoicism continues influencing contemporary thought and practice through these various channels, offering ancient and urgently relevant insights. Its presence in modern discourse is a testament to the timeless appeal of its core tenets—rationality, virtue, and resilience—which continue to offer guidance and solace in a complex world.

As this chapter draws to a close, we are reminded of the expansive reach and profound impact of Stoic philosophy from its ancient roots to its modern manifestations. Stoicism has not only survived the vicissitudes of history but has thrived, continually finding new expressions and applications that resonate with the challenges and aspirations of each era. As we transition to the next chapter, we carry forward the Stoic legacy of wisdom and virtue, exploring further how these ancient principles can continue to enrich our lives today.

Reflection Questions:

1. How does Stoicism define personal fulfillment and happiness?
2. In what ways can Stoic philosophy help you find purpose and meaning in your daily life?
3. How can practicing Stoic virtues contribute to a sense of personal fulfillment?

Journal Prompts:

1. Reflect on what personal fulfillment means to you. How can Stoic principles help you achieve this?
2. Write about a time when you felt truly content and fulfilled. What Stoic virtues were you practicing at that time?
3. Identify three areas where you can find greater fulfillment through applying Stoic philosophy. Develop a plan to incorporate these practices into your routine.

CHAPTER 8

STOIC EXERCISES FOR PERSONAL DEVELOPMENT

Imagine standing at the summit of a serene mountain, the vast landscape stretching endlessly before you. From this vantage point, bustling cities, winding rivers, and sprawling forests merge into a cohesive tapestry of the earth below. This perspective is not just transformative; it's revelatory. In Stoicism, we strive to achieve a similar outlook on our lives through a visualization technique that allows us to see things from a higher, more expansive view. This powerful exercise offers more than a mental respite—it profoundly shifts how we perceive our lives and the challenges we face.

8.1 '*The View from Above*': A Stoic Visualization Technique

Explanation of the Technique

This visualization practice encourages you to mentally ascend and look down upon your life from a distant, expansive perspective. Rooted in the Stoic principle that a broader view leads to a deeper understanding, it helps us see our lives as interconnected with others and part of a larger whole. By mentally distancing yourself from daily entanglements, you can perceive your problems not as consuming or insurmountable but as parts of a larger, manageable pattern.

Steps to Perform the Visualization

To effectively practice "The View from Above," follow these detailed steps, ensuring each phase contributes to deepening your understanding and perspective:

1. **Find a Quiet Space**: Begin by finding a quiet and comfortable place to sit or lie down without interruptions. This setting should feel safe and peaceful, conducive to deep thought and reflection.
2. **Focus on Breathing**: Close your eyes and take several deep, slow breaths. Concentrate on your breathing, feeling each breath filling your lungs and slowly leaving your body. This focus will help center your mind, making it receptive to visualization.
3. **Mentally Zoom Out**: Imagine yourself gradually rising above your current location, viewing the building, the street, and eventually the city from above. Continue this ascent until you see your region, country, and the earth from space.
4. Each stage should expand your perspective, making your concerns appear smaller and more contained.
5. **Reflect on Interconnectedness**: From this elevated viewpoint, reflect on how interconnected human experiences are and how your life is just one part of a vast, intricate system. Consider how your challenges and achievements are not just your own but part of a larger narrative that includes many lives and stories.

Benefits of this Technique

The psychological and emotional benefits of practicing "The View from Above" are manifold. Firstly, it provides enhanced perspective, allowing you to see your problems as more minor and less significant in the grand scheme of things, which can lead to reduced stress and anxiety. This broader viewpoint can also foster a greater sense of connection to humanity as you realize that your life is intertwined with those of others, sharing in a collective human experience.

Moreover, this practice can be particularly beneficial during intense stress or when facing difficult decisions. By distancing yourself from these high-pressure situations, you gain clarity as the emotional weight of the moment is diminished, allowing for more precise, more rational thinking. This detachment is not about disengagement but about gaining the freedom to assess situations objectively.

Examples of When to Use This Technique

Consider using this technique in various scenarios to enhance your understanding and decision-making:

During Personal or Professional Conflicts: When embroiled in conflict at home or work, use this visualization to gain a detached perspective. This will help you navigate the situation with less bias and emotion.

When Overwhelmed by Life's Pressures: When life's demands feel overwhelming, this practice can help you sort through your priorities by viewing your life from a broader perspective

Before Making Major Decisions: Before making significant life decisions, employ this technique to consider the broader implications of each option, aiding in more thoughtful and considered choices.

"The View from Above" is more than just a mental exercise; it is a portal to a new way of seeing the world and your place. Regularly engaging in this practice cultivates a mindset that appreciates the bigger picture, fostering resilience, empathy, and a profound sense of calm. As you continue to explore Stoic exercises for personal development, let this technique serve as a foundational tool, guiding you to greater clarity and peace in your journey through life.

8.2 Contemplating Impermanence for Inner Peace

In the tapestry of Stoic philosophy, impermanence holds a significant place, serving as a reminder of the ever-changing nature of existence. Stoicism teaches us that change is an inevitable reality and a fundamental aspect of the universe. Everything, from the smallest leaf to the mightiest empire, is subject to this universal law of change. Embracing this truth can lead to profound inner peace, as it aligns our expectations with the very nature of reality, encouraging a detachment from the fleeting and often illusory stability of material possessions and external conditions.

To truly understand and appreciate the role of impermanence in Stoic thought, consider how it contrasts with the pursuit of permanence that often characterizes modern life. The Stoic perspective offers a grounding counterpoint in a world with a continuous push toward acquiring more wealth, stability, and recognition. It teaches that this relentless pursuit can lead to great turmoil, as it goes against the fundamental grain of nature: change. By recognizing that nothing is permanent, you free yourself from the anxieties associated with loss and change, whether it's the end of a relationship, the obsolescence of technology, or the inevitable declines that come with aging.

Meditative Practice on Impermanence

To integrate the concept of impermanence into your life, begin with a simple meditative exercise. Find a quiet place where you can sit comfortably without interruptions. Close your eyes and take a few deep breaths, centering yourself in the present moment. Start by visualizing something simple, like a flower. Imagine it in its current state of blooming beauty. Slowly, let your mind's eye follow the natural progression of the flower's life—its eventual wilting, the petals falling away, and its return to the soil. Reflect on how this cycle of life and decay is natural, beautiful, and necessary. Then, gradually widen your meditation to include other aspects of your life—relationships, career, possessions—and reflect on how they, too, are transient. This practice helps in accepting the inevitability of change and appreciating the present moment, where the beauty of impermanence is often the most vivid.

How Contemplation Aids in Achieving Inner Peace

Regular contemplation of impermanence cultivates a mindset that expects and accepts change, crucial in mitigating fears and anxieties about the future. This acceptance does not mean passivity or resignation but a dynamic engagement with life, fully aware of the transient nature of all things. This awareness encourages you not to cling too tightly to current states or grieve too deeply over losses, as change is natural and universal. Such a perspective fosters a calm resilience, enabling you to face life's ups and downs with equanimity and grace.

Integrating Impermanence into Daily Life

To keep the awareness of impermanence active in your daily life, incorporate small practices that remind you of this crucial Stoic lesson. One effective method is daily mindfulness exercises focusing on the present moment. This could be as simple as paying close attention to the sensations of eating a meal or walking outside, noting the impermanent nature of these experiences. Another practice is to periodically declutter your living and working spaces, which can symbolize letting go, reinforcing the idea that holding on too tightly to possessions can hinder your appreciation of the present.

These practices, grounded in the Stoic tradition, offer more than philosophical insights—they provide practical tools for living a more fulfilled and peaceful life. As you continue to explore and apply the principles of Stoicism, let the contemplation of impermanence guide you, helping you navigate the complexities of existence with wisdom and tranquility. Through this understanding, you may find that life's transitory nature is not a source of fear but a cause for cherishing every moment with renewed vigor and appreciation.

8.3 The Practice of Premeditatio Malorum (Premeditation of Evils)

'Premeditatio Malorum' stands out as a profoundly pragmatic exercise in the rich tapestry of Stoic practices. It involves the foresighted anticipation of potential difficulties or misfortunes—not to dwell on fear but to prepare the mind to face adversities with composure and resilience. This Stoic exercise encourages contemplating possible future challenges in a controlled and rational manner, thus arming you with the mental fortitude to navigate them effectively when they arise.

The essence of Premeditatio Malorum lies in its capacity to transform your outlook on future uncertainties from dread to preparedness. By visualizing and mentally rehearsing how to handle potential adversities, you can significantly reduce anxiety about the unknown. This practice fosters a proactive mindset, shifting your approach from reactive to strategically anticipatory, empowering you to deal with potential setbacks with a calm and prepared disposition. Moreover, the regular practice of this technique enhances your resilience, enabling you to bounce back from setbacks more quickly and with more excellent emotional equilibrium.

To effectively practice Premeditatio Malorum, it is crucial to approach the exercise with balance and thoughtfulness to ensure it serves as a tool for empowerment rather than a source of undue stress. Here is a structured framework to guide you:

1. **Choose a Quiet Moment**: Set aside a calm, undistracted time to perform this exercise, ideally during a quiet part of your day when you can think clearly without interruptions.
2. **Identify Potential Challenges**: Reflect on upcoming events or general areas of difficulty. These could range from specific events, such as a major presentation at work or a family gathering, to general health or financial stability concerns.
3. **Visualize and Strategize**: For each identified challenge, vividly imagine how the scenario might unfold. See yourself encountering the difficulty, and focus on your reactions and decisions. Then, thoughtfully consider different strategies you might employ to manage or mitigate these challenges effectively.
4. **Emotional and Rational Preparation**: Consider your emotional responses as you visualize these challenges. Practice regulating your emotions and aligning your responses with Stoic principles of rationality and virtue. This part of the exercise is crucial as it prepares you to act with strategic foresight and emotional wisdom.

The real-life applications of Premeditatio Malorum are vast and varied, encompassing both professional and personal spheres. In a professional context, imagine you are preparing for an important project that involves numerous stakeholders. You can devise strategies in advance by anticipating potential disagreements or setbacks, such as building consensus through preliminary meetings or preparing backup plans. This preparation enables you to navigate the project with confidence and agility, significantly enhancing the likelihood of a successful outcome.

In your personal life, consider a scenario where you are dealing with a challenging relationship. By anticipating possible points of conflict and mentally preparing how you will handle them, you can ensure that when difficult conversations occur, you are more likely to respond with composure and empathy, preserving the relationship's integrity and deepening mutual understanding.

Premeditatio Malorum ("the premeditation of evils"), with its focus on foresight and preparedness, offers a robust method for enhancing your ability to handle life's uncertainties with grace and effectiveness. By regularly engaging in this practice, you cultivate a resilient and proactive mindset and a more profound confidence in your ability to manage whatever challenges life throws your way. Therefore, This Stoic exercise is not merely about preparing for adversities; it is about transforming how you engage with life, turning potential fears into opportunities for growth and learning.

As we close this chapter on Stoic exercises for personal development, remember that each technique provides unique tools for fostering resilience, wisdom, and peace. These practices are not just philosophical concepts but practical strategies that can profoundly influence how you navigate the complexities of modern life. Moving forward, let these exercises guide you in cultivating a life of virtue and fulfillment rooted deeply in the timeless wisdom of Stoicism.

Reflection Questions:

1. How does Stoicism enhance your understanding and management of emotions?
2. What are the key components of emotional intelligence, and how can Stoic practices help develop them?
3. How can Stoicism help you build stronger, more empathetic relationships?

Journal Prompts:

1. Reflect on a recent emotional experience. How could you have used Stoic techniques to understand and manage your emotions better?
2. Write about a relationship that could benefit from greater emotional intelligence. How can you apply Stoic principles to improve this relationship?
3. Identify a situation where you struggled to control your emotions. How can practicing Stoic virtues help you respond more effectively in the future?

CHAPTER 9

THE ETHICS OF STOICISM

In an era marked by divisions, where the global village often seems more like a series of isolated enclaves, Stoicism emerges as a personal philosophy and a blueprint for fostering a broader, more inclusive worldview. This chapter explores the Stoic concept of cosmopolitanism, a principle that champions universal brotherhood and ethical consistency, transcending geographic and cultural boundaries. Here, we delve into how this ancient idea is profoundly relevant today. We offer a perspective that might help bridge divides and foster a global community rooted in mutual respect and justice.

9.1 Universal Ethics and the Stoic Idea of Cosmopolitanism

Defining Stoic Cosmopolitanism

Imagine a world where every individual, regardless of nationality, culture, or religion, is viewed not as a foreigner but as a fellow citizen of the world. This is the essence of Stoic cosmopolitanism. Stemming from the

Greek word 'kosmopolitês,' meaning 'citizen of the cosmos,' this concept challenges us to consider ourselves members of a single, universal community. The Stoics first introduced this radical concept, particularly by Diogenes the Cynic, and later expanded upon by Marcus Aurelius. It invites us to shift our allegiance from local or national identities to a broader, all-encompassing identity that binds all humanity.

This Stoic principle is not merely about global awareness; it's a call to profound ethical commitment. It urges us to extend our concern, compassion, and moral obligations to every human being, treating all as we would treat members of our community. This universal approach to ethics is rooted in the Stoic belief in all humans' inherent rationality and dignity. This shared divine spark obliges us to act towards others with justice and kindness, irrespective of their external differences.

Philosophical Foundations of Universal Ethics

At the core of Stoic cosmopolitanism lies the belief in a common rationality that binds humanity. Stoics argue that this shared aspect of human nature establishes a moral obligation to treat everyone justly and compassionately. Just as the laws of physics are universal, so are the principles of ethical conduct in Stoicism. This universalism is grounded in the Stoic concept of 'logos,' the rational principle that pervades the universe and is inherent in all rational beings. By recognizing this shared rationality, we acknowledge that every person is capable of virtue and deserves respect and ethical treatment.

This perspective challenges us to expand our circle of concern beyond our immediate surroundings and personal relationships. It calls for an empathetic understanding that others share the same basic desires for happiness, freedom from suffering, and a meaningful life, no matter how distant or different. This Stoic view fosters a proactive stance on global ethics, advocating for actions that support our well-being and the well-being of others across the globe.

Practical Implications of Stoic Cosmopolitanism

Applying Stoic cosmopolitanism in today's world has profound implications for contemporary issues such as global justice, immigration, and international relations. For instance, in the face of global challenges like climate change, a Stoic might advocate for policies that consider the welfare of the entire planet, transcending nationalistic priorities to address a threat that affects all humanity.

Regarding immigration, Stoic cosmopolitanism would argue against policies that treat migrants as 'others,' advocating instead for policies that recognize all individuals' fundamental dignity and rights, regardless of origin. This application of Stoic principles to real-world issues can help us feel more engaged and connected to the material, seeing its relevance and potential impact.

This inclusive approach also invites us to rethink international relations, promoting cooperation over conflict and mutual benefit over zero-sum competition. It encourages a global perspective on economics, politics, and culture that seeks to harmonize different interests and values, fostering a world where diverse communities can coexist and thrive. By emphasizing the practical implications of Stoic cosmopolitanism, we can inspire and motivate the audience to apply these principles in their own lives, fostering a sense of personal growth and contribution to a more just and compassionate world.

Challenges and Critiques of Stoic Cosmopolitanism

Despite its ideals, implementing Stoic cosmopolitanism is challenging. Critics argue that prioritizing a global community might conflict with local duties and responsibilities. For instance, can one justify redirecting resources from one's community to help distant others, or does this betray a responsibility to those closest to us? Moreover, the practicality of universal moral obligations can be daunting in complex political, social, and economic systems. By acknowledging these challenges and critiques, we can make the audience feel understood and validated in their concerns, fostering a sense of open dialogue and mutual respect.

These critiques require carefully considering the balance between global ethical obligations and local duties. They challenge us to find practical ways to enact Stoic ideals without neglecting the immediate needs of our communities. This balancing act is not simple, but it is a crucial dialogue for Stoics and non-Stoics alike as we navigate the complexities of our interconnected world.

In engaging with these ideas, we are called upon to expand our horizons and consider our actions' immediate and global implications. Stoic cosmopolitanism doesn't just offer a way to think about the world; it provides a way to change it, urging us to act with justice, compassion, and respect for all. Reflecting on this profound Stoic principle, consider how you might embody these ideals daily, contributing to a more just and compassionate world.

9.2 Stoic Thoughts on Personal Integrity and Honesty

The Foundations of Integrity and Honesty in Stoicism

In Stoic philosophy, integrity and honesty are not just virtues but the very pillars that uphold a moral life. These qualities are closely connected to the Stoic aim of living in harmony with nature and reason. Integrity, for the Stoic, means aligning one's actions with one's values, ensuring a consistent and unwavering commitment to truth in all aspects of life. Honesty involves a firm dedication to truthfulness, which is essential for building trust and fostering authentic relationships.

Aligning Actions with Universal Reason (Logos)

Living with integrity and honesty, in the Stoic sense, means ensuring that one's actions are in harmony with the universal reason (Logos) that governs the world. This alignment leads to thoughtful responses that are rooted in rational understanding and ethical principles, rather than being mere reactions to external events. For example, in professional settings, maintaining integrity might involve refusing to engage in unethical practices, even if they are profitable. Such commitment to ethics, even at personal cost, strengthens one's character and earns lasting respect.

The Role of Honesty in Daily Interactions

Honesty in daily life is more than just avoiding lies; it involves being transparent about your intentions and feelings, and communicating them clearly. This level of honesty deepens relationships and helps prevent misunderstandings that could lead to conflict. For instance, being upfront about your capabilities and time constraints in a team project can set realistic expectations and foster a collaborative environment. Similarly, being open about your feelings and concerns can strengthen personal bonds and build mutual trust.

The Importance of Self-Examination

Regular self-examination is crucial for maintaining the virtues of integrity and honesty. Stoicism encourages ongoing self-assessment, where individuals reflect on their thoughts, decisions, and actions to ensure they align with Stoic principles. Tools like reflective journaling or evening reviews are valuable for this purpose. By consistently examining your behavior and motivations, you can identify any gaps between your professed values and your actual practices. This continuous scrutiny not only reveals areas for improvement but also reinforces your commitment to living a virtuous life.

Historical and Contemporary Examples of Stoic Integrity

Throughout history, many individuals have embodied Stoic integrity and honesty. A notable example is Cato the Younger, a Roman statesman famous for his unwavering integrity and resistance to corruption. Despite the moral decline of the late Roman Republic, Cato remained steadfast in his principles, often at great personal and political cost. His life illustrates the Stoic belief that true happiness and respect are found in living a life of virtue, rather than in seeking material gain or popularity.

The Relevance of Stoic Virtues Today

In modern times, examples of Stoic integrity can be seen in leaders and public figures who stand firm in their ethical convictions, even when under pressure to compromise. Whistleblowers in corporate and governmental contexts, for instance, often risk their careers and personal well-being to expose wrongdoing and uphold the truth. Their actions, driven by a commitment to honesty and justice, reflect the Stoic ideal of living by one's principles, regardless of the consequences.

The Timeless Impact of Stoic Virtues

Both ancient and modern examples highlight the enduring relevance of living with Stoic integrity and honesty. They remind us that true success is not measured by external achievements but by adherence to ethical values, which commands respect and leads to a meaningful life. As you navigate the complexities of contemporary life, consider how the Stoic virtues of integrity and honesty can guide your decisions and interactions, shaping a life that is not only successful but also deeply respected and fulfilling.

9.3 The Stoic Approach to Wealth and Possessions

Understanding Wealth as 'Indifferent' in Stoicism

In Stoic philosophy, material wealth is categorized as 'indifferent,' meaning it is neither inherently good nor bad. This term does not suggest that wealth is unimportant but rather that it lacks intrinsic moral value. The true worth of wealth is determined by how it is used—whether to promote virtue or vice. This perspective offers a nuanced approach to financial resources, emphasizing that wealth can contribute to a good life if used ethically. However, it should not be the basis of one's happiness or self-worth.

Using Wealth as a Tool for Virtue

For Stoics, the true measure of wealth lies not in the accumulation of possessions but in the cultivation of virtue. Wealth becomes valuable when it serves as a tool for doing good, such as supporting family, helping the less fortunate, funding education, or advancing community projects. This ethical use of wealth aligns with the Stoic commitment to living in accordance with nature, which includes the well-being of our fellow humans. Consider, for example, a business owner who allocates part of their profits to fund local scholarships. Such actions exemplify the Stoic approach to wealth, where financial success is directed toward uplifting others and aligning personal prosperity with communal progress.

The Moral Hazards Associated with Wealth

Despite its potential for good, the pursuit and possession of wealth come with significant moral risks. Stoicism warns against allowing wealth to become the central focus of life. Greed, envy, and corruption often accompany wealth, leading individuals away from virtue and toward harmful actions. The Stoic philosopher Epictetus cautioned that wealth can create a false sense of security and self-importance, distracting individuals from moral and spiritual development. Stoics, therefore, maintain a vigilant attitude toward wealth, ensuring it remains a servant rather than a master in one's life.

The Stoic Solution: Simplicity and Self-Sufficiency

To counter the dangers associated with wealth, Stoics advocate for simplicity and self-sufficiency. By limiting desires to what is necessary and sufficient for a good life, one reduces the risk of moral corruption and maintains freedom from the undue influence of wealth. This practice of simplicity is not about austerity for its own sake but about prioritizing internal wealth—qualities like wisdom, courage, justice, and temperance—over external accumulations.

Exemplars of Stoic Simplicity

The lifestyle of Stoic simplicity is vividly illustrated in the lives of individuals like Zeno of Citium, the founder of Stoicism, who famously eschewed luxury in favor of a life rich in philosophical pursuits and community involvement. In contemporary times, individuals such as Warren Buffett, known for his modest lifestyle despite immense wealth, embody Stoic principles. Buffett's pledge to donate most of his wealth to philanthropy reflects a commitment to using financial resources for the greater good rather than personal indulgence, aligning closely with Stoic ideals.

Reflecting on Your Relationship with Wealth

When considering the Stoic approach to wealth, it's important to reflect on how your relationship with money aligns with your values and virtues. Does your pursuit of financial success support your moral and ethical goals, or does it detract from them? Are your possessions a means to an end, or have they become ends in themselves? Regularly assessing how you acquire and use wealth can help ensure that your financial decisions enhance rather than compromise your ability to live a virtuous life.

Wealth and Virtue in Stoic Philosophy

This exploration of Stoic ethics regarding wealth and possessions demonstrates that Stoicism offers both philosophical insights and practical guidance for navigating modern economic life. By viewing wealth through the lens of indifference, balanced by a commitment to virtue, you can use your financial resources wisely, ensuring they contribute to a life that is not only prosperous but also profoundly meaningful and aligned with the greater good.

Reflection Questions

1. What does resilience mean in the context of Stoic philosophy?
2. How can Stoic practices help you build mental and emotional resilience?
3. What are some common obstacles to resilience, and how can you overcome them using Stoic principles?

Journal Prompts

1. Reflect on a challenging time in your life. How did you demonstrate resilience, and how could Stoic principles have further supported you?
2. Develop a personal resilience plan based on Stoic practices. What specific actions will you take to strengthen your resilience?
3. Write about a situation where you felt overwhelmed. How can you build resilience to better handle similar situations in the future?

CHAPTER 10

STOICISM AND EMOTIONAL WELLNESS

In the tapestry of our lives, woven with diverse experiences and challenges, emotional wellness often emerges as both a fundamental pursuit and a pervasive challenge. Amidst this, Stoicism serves not merely as a philosophical beacon but as a practical toolkit, adeptly addressing the nuances of modern emotional complexities. This chapter delves into the Stoic methodology for managing two of the most common emotional disturbances that unsettle the human spirit: anxiety and fear. We explore not only the Stoic perspective on these emotions but also practical exercises and strategies designed to transform them from overwhelming forces into sources of personal growth and resilience.

10.1 Stoic Techniques for Anxiety and Fear

Understanding Anxiety Through a Stoic Lens

From a Stoic viewpoint, anxiety and fear are not triggered by external events themselves but by our perceptions and interpretations of these events. This distinction is both crucial and liberating, shifting the battlefield from the unpredictability of the external world to the more controllable realm of our internal thoughts. Stoicism teaches us that we can maintain our tranquility by changing our responses, not the circumstances. For instance, a job loss, public criticism, or personal failure can trigger anxiety, while a sudden threat or danger can lead to fear. Understanding these perspectives helps us manage these emotions more effectively.

The Stoic practice of differentiating between what we can control—our thoughts, perceptions, and actions—and what we cannot—the vast array of external events—is vital. This discernment is not about withdrawal but about redirecting our focus toward areas where we have true agency. For example, you might not control the economic fluctuations that impact your business, but you can control your response to these challenges, choosing proactive engagement over reactive anxiety.

Practical Stoic Exercises to Manage Anxiety

One of the most potent Stoic exercises for managing anxiety is the *premeditatio malorum*, or the premeditation of future difficulties. This practice involves contemplating potential adverse events and visualizing how to handle them stoically. By mentally rehearsing your responses to scenarios such as job loss, public criticism, or personal failure, you reduce the shock and paralysis that such events might cause if they occur unexpectedly.

This exercise builds psychological resilience, empowering you to face adversity in a controlled, thoughtful manner, thus diminishing the fear and anxiety associated with potential negative outcomes. In essence, it's about preparing your mind for the worst so you're not caught off guard if it happens.

Another significant Stoic tool is cognitive reframing, which involves changing your perspective on anxiety-inducing situations to see them as opportunities for personal growth and the practice of virtue. For instance, viewing a challenging project not as a threat but as a chance to enhance your skills and resilience can transform anxiety into motivation, channeling your energy into productive action rather than worry.

Use of Stoic Affirmations to Counter Fear

Stoic affirmations are simple yet powerful tools that reinforce the philosophy's principles and fortify the mind against anxiety and fear. Consider the words of Marcus Aurelius: "The impediment to action advances action. What stands in the way becomes the way." By repeating such affirmations, you remind yourself that obstacles are not just barriers but invitations to strengthen your virtues, such as courage, perseverance, and adaptability.

Other affirmations like "I am prepared for whatever comes my way" or "I am in control of my thoughts and actions" can also serve as mental anchors, keeping you steadfast in your Stoic practice and mindset, especially when fear threatens to unsettle your peace. These affirmations instill a sense of confidence in your ability to overcome challenges.

Long-term Strategies for Reducing Anxiety

The long-term Stoic strategy for managing anxiety involves a consistent practice of focusing on present actions and maintaining an awareness of life's impermanence. This approach encourages you to live fully in the present, engaging deeply with your current tasks and interactions without the distracting worry about the past or future. It also cultivates an acceptance of life's transient nature, which helps release irrational fears about change and loss, grounding you in the enduring flow of now and bringing a profound sense of peace.

By integrating these Stoic techniques into your daily life, you can gradually transform anxiety into empowerment and equanimity. This transformation is not instantaneous but develops through persistent practice as you learn to apply Stoic wisdom in moments of calm and, crucially, in times of challenge and uncertainty. Through this ongoing practice, you not only manage anxiety and fear more effectively but also enhance your overall emotional wellness, fostering a life characterized not by the absence of difficulties but by the graceful and virtuous manner in which you navigate them.

10.2 Overcoming Anger through Stoic Mindfulness

Understanding Anger as a Disturbance

In the Stoic framework, anger is viewed not as a fundamental aspect of human nature but rather as a disturbance of the mind that arises from faulty judgments. The Stoics believed that true rationality could prevent anger's onset by correcting these misjudgments at their root. This perspective holds that every instance of anger results from an incorrect belief about the necessity of the emotion in response to a particular stimulus. For example, if someone believes that an insult diminishes their personal value, they are likely to respond with anger. However, if they understand that their value is independent of others' opinions, their response can remain calm and untroubled.

Stoic Mindfulness Techniques

Stoic mindfulness, particularly in managing anger, involves a series of deliberate techniques to foster a deep, objective awareness of one's emotional state. This begins with cultivating an observational stance towards one's feelings, where emotions are seen not as imperatives to action but as phenomena to be studied. This detachment allows for a space between feeling anger and acting upon it, providing a moment for reason to reassume control.

For instance, when a surge of anger arises due to a perceived injustice at work, you might pause to observe this anger, noting its intensity and the bodily sensations it engenders instead of immediately reacting. This pause is crucial—you can ask yourself whether this anger is based on a correct perception of the situation or whether it results from a mistaken judgment about what is truly good or bad for you.

Empathy as a Tool for Diffusing Anger

Empathy plays an essential role in this context. Stoicism encourages the development of empathy through exercises that help you consider situations from others' perspectives, thereby reducing the likelihood of misinterpretation that often leads to anger. Suppose a colleague fails to meet a project deadline. Before anger can take root, consider potential reasons from their perspective—perhaps they are dealing with personal issues, or maybe there was a miscommunication about the deadline. This shift in viewpoint can transform anger into understanding, fostering a more supportive work environment and reducing the potential for conflict.

Daily Practices to Reduce Anger

Daily Stoic practices can be instrumental in systematically reducing occurrences of anger. For example, journaling is a powerful tool for reflecting on incidents that trigger anger. By writing about these events and describing what happened, how you responded, and what you might do differently, you gain clarity and insight into your anger triggers and habitual responses to them. This reflective process encourages a more mindful, controlled approach to such situations in the future.

Here's a practical exercise: at the end of each day, jot down any moments when you felt anger, however minor. Describe the scenario and your immediate response, then reflect on how a Stoic might interpret the same situation. Could there have been a misunderstanding? What might have been unknown factors affecting the other person's behavior? This practice deepens your understanding of Stoic principles and embeds them into your daily emotional responses, paving the way for a more reasoned and serene approach to life's inevitable provocations.

Through these practices—mindful observation, empathetic consideration, and reflective journaling—you gradually cultivate a disposition that is less prone to anger and more aligned with Stoic equanimity. This transformation does not occur overnight, nor does it mean you will never feel angry again. Instead, it signifies a profound shift in how you experience and respond to anger, turning reactive impulses into opportunities for virtue and growth. As you continue to integrate these Stoic techniques into your life, you may find that situations that once sparked anger now evoke a more measured, compassionate, and rational response, reflecting not only your mastery of Stoic mindfulness but also your deepening commitment to living a life guided by reason and virtue.

10.3 The Stoic Path to Contentment and Happiness

Virtue as the Foundation of Happiness

Exploring the Stoic conception of happiness, or eudaimonia, it becomes evident that true contentment is derived not from the accumulation of material wealth or external accolades but from a life lived in harmony with virtue and reason. Stoicism teaches that happiness is achieved through the cultivation of the soul's excellences—virtues that align our actions with the rational order of the universe. This profound understanding suggests that contentment is not a fleeting sensation but a steadfast state achieved by aligning one's life with ethical principles.

The Role of Key Virtues

Virtues such as wisdom, justice, courage, and temperance are essential in fostering true happiness. Each virtue uniquely contributes to developing a well-rounded character, which is essential for navigating life's complexities with grace. Wisdom, for instance, enhances our ability to make decisions that resonate with our deepest values, while justice ensures that our actions contribute positively to the well-being of others, affirming our place within the community. Courage allows us to face life's inevitable challenges without succumbing to despair, and temperance provides the balance necessary to enjoy life's pleasures without being enslaved by them. Together, these virtues form a robust framework within which one can achieve not only momentary happiness but also enduring contentment.

Daily Practices for Cultivating Happiness

The Stoic pursuit of happiness involves daily practices that reinforce these virtues. Setting daily intentions based on virtuous actions is a powerful practice that focuses the mind on ethical goals rather than on uncontrolled outcomes. Each morning, consider the virtues you wish to cultivate and set specific, actionable intentions that align with these virtues. For example, if you choose to focus on justice, your intention might be to engage in an act of kindness that promotes fairness or to advocate for someone who may not have the means to advocate for themselves.

The Role of Gratitude and Community Service

Gratitude, too, plays a pivotal role in Stoic happiness. By regularly practicing gratitude for present conditions—regardless of whether they align perfectly with your desires—you train yourself to appreciate what you have rather than lament what you lack. This shift in focus from deficiency to abundance fosters a profound sense of contentment. Consider maintaining a gratitude journal where you record daily instances of thankfulness, no matter how small. This practice uplifts the spirit and shifts your perspective from one of scarcity to one of abundance.

Engaging in community service is another practical way to embody Stoic principles and enhance your sense of happiness. Stoicism posits that humans are inherently social creatures meant to contribute to the common welfare of their community. By participating in activities that help others—whether through volunteer work, mentorship, or simple acts of kindness—you experience the joy of making a meaningful impact, deepening your sense of purpose and fulfillment.

Facing Life's Challenges with Stoic Resilience

Despite these pathways to happiness, Stoicism acknowledges life's inevitable challenges—societal pressures, personal setbacks, and the unpredictable nature of human existence. However, it equips you with the philosophical tools to overcome these obstacles. Stoic resilience lies not in denying these challenges but in facing them with a mindset that views every difficulty as an opportunity for growth and reaffirming virtue.

When faced with setbacks, remind yourself of the impermanence of all things and focus on maintaining your commitment to virtuous living. This perspective alleviates the sting of adverse events and positions you to emerge from challenges with greater wisdom and strength.

As we conclude this exploration of Stoic happiness, it becomes clear that the path to true contentment is continuous personal and moral development. Stoicism doesn't promise an easy life but offers a profoundly rewarding one, rich with opportunities for personal growth and the joy that comes from living in accordance with deep ethical convictions.

In the next chapter, we will continue to explore how Stoic principles can be applied to foster robust relationships, further enhancing our understanding of how Stoicism serves as a personal guide and a blueprint for enriching interactions with others.

Reflection Questions:

1. How does Stoicism relate to modern concepts of mindfulness?
2. What are the benefits of practicing mindfulness from a Stoic perspective?
3. How can you incorporate Stoic mindfulness practices into your daily routine?

Journal Prompts:

1. Reflect on a moment when you felt completely present and mindful. How can you recreate this state using Stoic principles?
2. Write about a daily activity that you often perform mindlessly. How can you bring more mindfulness to this activity using Stoic techniques?
3. Develop a mindfulness routine based on Stoic practices. What specific exercises or reflections will you include?

CHAPTER 11

STOICISM IN PERSONAL RELATIONSHIPS

Stoicism and the Art of Loving Wisely

In the labyrinth of human relationships, navigating love and partnership with wisdom and grace is one of life's most challenging quests. Stoicism, a philosophy renowned for its resilience and profound insights into human nature, offers valuable guidance on cultivating meaningful, enduring partnerships. Imagine love not merely as a sentiment but as a shared journey toward virtue, where each person supports the other's highest good—a concept deeply rooted in Stoic philosophy.

11.1 Stoic Advice on Love and Partnership

Understanding Love Through a Stoic Lens

Stoicism teaches that true love is grounded in mutual respect and shared virtue. In Stoicism, 'virtue' refers to qualities such as wisdom, courage, justice, and temperance—qualities that Stoics believe lead to a good life. Love, in this context, is not based on transient emotions or superficial attractions, but on a shared commitment to these virtues. This perspective views love as a partnership where individuals actively support each other's moral and personal growth, encouraging one another to live their best lives. Such a relationship is built on the pillars of honesty, integrity, and a deep commitment to mutual well-being, aligning closely with the Stoic ideal of living in harmony with nature and reason.

In this Stoic framework, love is not merely about personal fulfillment but about forming a union that fosters virtue and wisdom in both partners. For example, a Stoic approach to love involves encouraging a partner to pursue their personal and professional goals, even when this requires sacrifice or compromise. This supportive dynamic ensures that the relationship contributes positively to both individuals' well-being and moral development, making it a true partnership in the fullest sense.

Maintaining Equanimity in Relationships

One of the central tenets of Stoicism is maintaining equanimity—calmness and composure—amid life's inevitable ups and downs. In the context of relationships, this means managing emotions to promote harmony and understanding. Stoicism advocates a balanced approach to emotions, encouraging a state that is neither overly detached nor excessively passionate. This equanimity is achieved through mindfulness and reflective meditation, which help individuals observe their feelings without being overwhelmed. It's about maintaining a calm and rational mindset, even in the face of challenging situations, to ensure that your actions are guided by reason rather than emotion.

For instance, in moments of conflict or disagreement within a relationship, you might take a step back to assess the situation calmly rather than reacting impulsively with anger or frustration. By doing so, you can respond in a way that addresses the issue without harming the relationship, embodying the Stoic ideal of responding to external events with internal wisdom.

The Role of Self-Sufficiency in Partnerships

Stoicism places high value on personal self-sufficiency, which refers to finding contentment and peace within oneself without undue reliance on external sources. In relationships, this principle does not imply emotional distance or isolation; rather, it enhances the quality of the relationship by reducing dependency and fostering a healthy, balanced dynamic. When both partners are self-sufficient, the relationship is based on choice rather than need, significantly strengthening the bond and ensuring that both individuals contribute positively to each other's lives.

Emphasizing self-sufficiency means recognizing that while your partner enhances your life, your happiness and well-being are ultimately your responsibilities. This mindset encourages both partners to maintain their individuality and pursue personal growth, even while they grow together as a couple. This balanced approach prevents co-dependency and nurtures a relationship where both partners are whole, content individuals who choose to share their lives out of love and mutual respect.

Practical Exercises for Couples

To strengthen the bonds of partnership through Stoic practices, consider engaging in these exercises together:

Shared Meditations on Gratitude: Regularly set aside time to meditate together on the aspects of your life and relationship for which you are grateful. This practice fosters a positive outlook and deepens your appreciation for each other and the life you share.

Joint Reflections on Virtues: Discuss and reflect on how you can incorporate Stoic virtues such as courage, temperance, justice, and wisdom into your daily lives. For instance, courage can be seen in the face of adversity, temperance in the moderation of desires, justice in fair and honest dealings, and wisdom in making sound decisions. This exercise promotes personal growth and aligns your actions and decisions with shared ethical values.

Discussions on Supporting Each Other's Growth: Discuss your personal goals and how you can support each other in achieving them. This can involve setting shared goals, offering encouragement during challenges, or providing constructive feedback.

These exercises enrich your relationship and embed Stoic principles into your daily interactions, helping you grow individually and as a couple. Through these practices, you can build a partnership that not only withstands the tests of time but also flourishes in virtue and mutual support. As you continue to explore and apply Stoic wisdom in your relationships, remember that each step taken together is a step towards a more profound and fulfilling union.

11.2 Dealing with Difficult People: A Stoic Strategy

Navigating Interpersonal Challenges with Stoicism

As we navigate the complex tapestry of human interactions, encountering individuals who challenge our patience and composure is inevitable. Stoicism, with its rich reservoir of wisdom on maintaining inner peace and rationality, provides invaluable strategies for dealing with difficult people. By adopting Stoic methods, you can not only navigate but also transform potentially disruptive encounters into opportunities for personal growth and virtue cultivation, empowering you to remain in control of your reactions.

Understanding and Empathy in Conflict

Stoicism teaches us to approach interpersonal conflicts with a mindset of understanding and rational response. When faced with complex individuals, whether in professional settings or personal relationships, the philosophy encourages us first to seek to understand the perspectives of others. This understanding does not imply agreement but recognizes that each person's behavior and reactions are driven by their judgments and perceptions, which they believe to be true. Acknowledging this, you can interact with challenging individuals without immediate emotional engagement, maintaining your composure and focusing on thoughtful dialogue.

The importance of empathy and patience cannot be overstated in these interactions. Stoicism promotes empathy as a tool for deeper understanding and effective communication. It teaches that everyone, no matter how difficult they seem, acts according to what they believe is right, often based on misguided judgments or lack of knowledge. By practicing empathy, you strive to see the situation from the other person's perspective, which can provide insights into why they act the way they do and how best to respond. Patience complements empathy by allowing you time to choose your responses carefully, ensuring they are aligned with Stoic virtues and conducive to resolving conflict rather than escalating it.

Practical Exercises for Dealing with Difficult People

Cultivating empathy and patience can be enhanced through specific Stoic exercises. One effective practice is the discipline of assent, where you withhold immediate judgment and reaction to another's actions, giving yourself the space to analyze and understand the situation more fully. Another valuable exercise is the contemplation of the interconnectedness of all people, which fosters a deeper appreciation for the shared human experience, even with those who challenge us.

Moreover, Stoicism encourages us to reframe challenges as opportunities for growth. Interacting with difficult people provides a real-life arena to practice virtues such as temperance, which involves moderating our reactions and maintaining self-control, and grit, the courage to uphold your values despite external pressures. Each complex interaction becomes a lesson in virtue, a chance to strengthen your character in the face of adversity. This perspective shifts your focus from the stress of the conflict to the personal gains in wisdom and resilience, making the encounter more tolerable and potentially rewarding.

Historical Examples and Modern Application

Historical examples abound of Stoics who managed relationships with difficult people effectively. Consider the philosopher Epictetus, who, despite his enslavement, maintained a perspective that saw challenges as opportunities to practice his philosophy. His teachings emphasize the power of choice in responding to others, suggesting that true freedom comes from within and cannot be hindered by external difficulties. Another poignant example is Marcus Aurelius, whose reign as Roman Emperor involved interactions with various challenging figures, from political adversaries to betraying allies. His meditations reveal a continuous commitment to Stoic principles, using each complex interaction as a moment to practice patience, understanding, and strategic response.

In your daily life, when you encounter challenging individuals, try to see these interactions through the Stoic lens. Reflect on your experiences by journaling about encounters with difficult people and evaluating your responses based on Stoic virtues. Over time, this reflective practice can enhance your ability to remain calm and composed, turning every challenging interaction into a step toward becoming a more virtuous and resilient individual. As you implement these strategies, remember that each person you meet carries their struggles and judgments. Your responses not only define the quality of your interactions but also the quality of your character.

11.3 Teaching Children Stoic Principles

Introducing Stoicism to Children

Incorporating Stoic principles into parenting enriches your own life and profoundly influences your children, equipping them with tools to navigate their emotions and interactions effectively from a young age.

Introducing children to Stoicism involves more than teaching them philosophical concepts; it's about guiding them toward understanding and practicing virtues like self-control, fairness, and resilience in age-appropriate ways. This process begins with simple lessons in emotional regulation and ethical behavior, providing a foundation for more complex philosophical discussions as they grow.

The Concept of Control in Stoicism

The foundational aspect of teaching Stoicism to children is helping them understand what is within their control. This concept, central to Stoic philosophy, is vital for children as they learn to navigate their emotions and reactions. For instance, while they cannot control if it rains, affecting their playtime plans, they can control their response to such changes. Teaching this distinction helps children develop a sense of agency and reduces feelings of helplessness and frustration.

Begin by using simple, everyday examples to explain these concepts. Discuss scenarios that might affect their mood or day, like a change in plans or a disappointment, and explore different ways they could respond, emphasizing the healthier, more constructive choices. Introducing them to the idea of control over reactions also enhances their problem-solving skills. Additionally, instill the importance of honesty and fairness in their interactions. Use stories or role-playing games to illustrate these virtues, discussing the consequences of honesty versus deceit or fair versus unfair actions, making these abstract concepts tangible for young minds.

Stoic Exercises for Children

Practical exercises can effectively reinforce the Stoic teachings you introduce to your children. One simple exercise is to have them list things they can control and things they cannot at the end of each day. This could be part of a bedtime routine where you discuss the day's events and identify elements within and outside their control. Such reflective practices encourage children to internalize the concept of control, gradually applying it more broadly in their lives.

Another engaging exercise is reflecting on daily actions, which fosters self-awareness and personal responsibility. Encourage your child to think about their actions throughout the day and what they learned from them. For instance, if they helped a sibling or friend, discuss how that made them feel and what outcomes their actions had. Reinforcing positive behavior helps them see their impact on others, nurturing empathy and social responsibility.

The Role of the Parent as a Stoic Role Model

As a parent, your behavior and responses to challenges are powerful lessons for your children. Demonstrating Stoic principles in everyday actions allows children to see these philosophies in practice. When you respond to stress with composure or handle disputes with fairness, you embody the Stoic virtues, providing a live example for your children to emulate.

Share your challenges and how you apply Stoic principles to overcome them. If you had a difficult day at work, discuss it with your family during dinner, highlighting how you managed your emotions or resolved conflicts. This transparency strengthens your relationship with your children and teaches them practical applications of Stoicism in adult life.

Benefits of Stoic Principles in Children's Development

The benefits of integrating Stoic principles into children's development are extensive. Children cultivate emotional intelligence by learning to control their reactions, enabling them to handle their feelings and empathize with others effectively. The emphasis on fairness and honesty builds their moral compass, which guides them in making ethical decisions throughout their lives.

Furthermore, the Stoic focus on resilience—seeing obstacles as opportunities for growth—prepares children to face life's challenges with confidence and strength. This mindset encourages a proactive rather than reactive approach to problems, fostering a lifelong habit of seeking constructive solutions and personal growth.

By integrating these Stoic principles into your parenting, you enhance your children's emotional and ethical development and contribute to their overall well-being, preparing them to lead balanced, fulfilling lives. As you continue to guide them through these teachings, remember that every small step in teaching them about control, honesty, and resilience is a step toward nurturing a wise, virtuous, and resilient individual.

Reflection Questions:

1. How does Stoicism address the importance of physical health and well-being?
2. What Stoic practices can help you maintain and improve your physical health?
3. How can the mind-body connection be strengthened through Stoic philosophy?

Journal Prompts:

1. Reflect on your current physical health. How can Stoic principles help you achieve your health goals?
2. Write about a time when you faced a physical health challenge. How could Stoic practices have helped you cope better?

Create a plan to improve your physical health using Stoic principles. What specific actions will you take to incorporate Stoic virtues into your health routine?

CHAPTER 12

THE BROADER INFLUENCE OF STOICISM

In the ever-expanding garden of philosophy, where ideas blossom and intertwine, Stoicism is not a solitary bloom but part of a vibrant tapestry woven with threads from both Western and Eastern traditions. This chapter explores the rich, often overlooked parallels between Stoic philosophy and Eastern philosophies such as Buddhism and Taoism. Though these traditions may seem distant in origin and practice, they converge in profound ways, enhancing our understanding of the mind, ethics, and the universe. By examining these intersections, we deepen our comprehension of Stoicism and appreciate its versatile applicability in diverse cultural contexts, ultimately enhancing mental and spiritual well-being.

12.1 Stoicism and its Parallels with Eastern Philosophies

Comparative Analysis with Eastern Philosophies

At first glance, Stoicism and Eastern philosophies like Buddhism and Taoism might appear distinct. Stoicism, rooted in the rationalism of the Hellenistic period, emphasizes logical analysis and the importance of virtue grounded in reason. In contrast, Eastern philosophies often focus on intuition, meditation, and the transcendence of dualistic thinking. However, a deeper exploration reveals striking similarities, particularly in their approaches to mindfulness, detachment, and understanding the nature of suffering.

Understanding Suffering in Stoicism and Buddhism

Both Stoicism and Buddhism stress the importance of understanding the root causes of human suffering. Stoicism teaches that suffering arises from our desires and aversions to things outside our control—a perspective that echoes the Buddhist teaching of the Second Noble Truth, which states that suffering is caused by desire. Similarly, both philosophies advocate for a form of detachment—not as a way to disengage from the world, but as a means to achieve inner peace and ethical living. In Stoicism, the focus is on accepting only what is within our control, while in Buddhism, there is a cultivation of non-attachment to transient states and things.

Influence on Integrative Philosophical Practices

The synergies between Stoicism and Eastern philosophies have inspired integrative practices that combine elements from both traditions to address contemporary spiritual and psychological needs. Mindfulness meditation, though rooted in Buddhist tradition, shares common ground with the Stoic exercise of reflective meditation, where one examines thoughts and actions on a daily basis. Both practices cultivate a heightened awareness of the present moment, encouraging a state of calm observation that allows for emotional regulation and deeper engagement with life.

In therapeutic settings, these integrated practices are increasingly utilized to help individuals manage stress, anxiety, and personal crises. Techniques that combine Stoic rationalism with Buddhist mindfulness assist individuals in understanding the sources of their emotional disturbances and developing practical skills to manage them effectively. This holistic approach fosters resilience, deeply informed by philosophical wisdom and practical adaptability.

Shared Ethical and Metaphysical Concepts

One of the most profound areas of convergence between Stoicism and Eastern philosophies lies in their shared ethical and metaphysical concepts. Both traditions emphasize living in harmony with the universe—Stoicism through the concept of Logos, which represents rational divine order, and Taoism through the Tao, which signifies the fundamental nature of the universe as balanced and harmonious. These concepts encourage a life aligned with the natural world, advocating for actions consistent with universal virtues such as balance, moderation, and compassion.

Practical Applications in Cross-Cultural Contexts

Stoicism and Eastern philosophies are not just theoretical constructs; they have practical applications that are varied and impactful in cross-cultural settings. For instance, in spiritual retreats, elements of Stoic philosophy are often integrated with Taoist and Buddhist practices to help participants develop greater emotional intelligence and spiritual awareness. These retreats might combine Stoic teachings on virtue and self-control with Taoist principles of harmony and flow, providing a rich, multifaceted experience that supports individuals' holistic development. Such practical approaches can inspire you to explore these philosophies in your own life and witness their positive impact on your personal growth.

Moreover, facilitators increasingly blend these philosophies in personal development workshops to help attendees navigate life's challenges with grace and wisdom. Through exercises that foster Stoic resilience and Buddhist mindfulness, participants learn to manage their responses to external stresses, leading to more fulfilling and balanced lives.

Integrating Stoicism with Eastern Philosophies

In exploring these philosophical intersections, you are invited to see Stoicism not just as a self-contained system, but as part of a global dialogue that enriches our understanding and application of its principles. Integrating these insights into your life can serve as tools for personal growth and as bridges to a broader world of philosophical practice, where East meets West in the quest for wisdom and tranquility.

12.2 The Stoic Roots of Modern Self-Help Trends

Historical Influence of Stoicism on Self-Help Literature

The vast and ever-growing field of self-help literature contains profound echoes of Stoic philosophy. Tracing its influence from the intellectual rejuvenation during the Renaissance to the self-help boom of the 20th and 21st centuries, Stoicism has significantly shaped modern approaches to personal development, resilience, and happiness. This influence is not recent; it has deep historical roots that connect modern self-help literature to a rich intellectual tradition. The thematic content of today's self-help literature, along with the strategies it advocates for managing life's challenges, are deeply influenced by Stoic philosophy.

The Renaissance and Enlightenment Connection

Historically, the reintroduction of Stoic texts during the Renaissance sparked renewed interest in its practical applications. Thinkers like Erasmus of Rotterdam and later Michel de Montaigne drew heavily on Stoic philosophy, integrating its principles into their writings, which questioned human existence, virtue, and happiness. Their works laid the groundwork for later philosophers and writers, creating a path to modern self-help literature. By the time of the Enlightenment, Stoicism was firmly embedded in the intellectual landscape, influencing seminal thinkers such as Immanuel Kant and Adam Smith. Their ideas have permeated various self-help approaches, focusing on moral righteousness and the economic and social well-being of the individual.

Contemporary Stoicism in Self-Help Literature

In contemporary times, Stoic philosophy has found robust expression in the self-help genre, with authors like Ryan Holiday and William B. Irvine exploring Stoic principles in the context of modern challenges. These contemporary interpretations emphasize core Stoic concepts such as controlling one's response to external events, practicing mindfulness, and pursuing personal virtue. For example, the Stoic focus on controlling only what is within our power has been widely adopted in self-help literature to combat feelings of helplessness and overwhelm in the face of life's uncontrollable circumstances. This idea encourages a proactive rather than reactive approach to life's challenges, empowering individuals to take charge of their actions and attitudes.

Stoic Mindfulness in Modern Self-Help

Moreover, the Stoic practice of mindfulness—which involves a conscious awareness of one's thoughts and actions in the present moment—has been integrated into numerous self-help books and wellness programs. This practice is not just a philosophical concept but a practical tool that can significantly improve mental health and overall life satisfaction. By fostering disciplined attention to the present, individuals learn to disengage from past regrets and future anxieties. This technique can motivate you to incorporate Stoic mindfulness into your daily life, enhancing your concentration, reducing stress, and promoting a more profound sense of peace.

Analysis of Popular Self-Help Books with Stoic Principles

A closer look at several best-selling self-help books reveals a consistent integration of Stoic principles tailored to address modern-day issues. Books such as *The Obstacle Is the Way* by Ryan Holiday explicitly draw on Stoicism to frame challenges as opportunities for growth. Holiday interprets the Stoic practice of turning obstacles into advantages, illustrating through historical and contemporary examples how perceived setbacks can be transformed into stepping stones for success. Similarly, *How to Think Like a Roman Emperor* by Donald Robertson weaves cognitive behavioral therapy with Stoic philosophy, offering readers practical exercises to improve emotional resilience and psychological well-being, reflecting the Stoic idea that our emotions follow our judgments and perceptions.

Critique of Stoicism's Adaptation in Self-Help

While the adaptation of Stoic principles has undoubtedly enriched the self-help genre, offering robust methodologies for personal development and emotional resilience, it also has its drawbacks. In some instances, Stoic philosophy is oversimplified in the self-help context, reduced to catchy maxims or quick-fix solutions that overlook Stoicism's philosophical depth and complexity. This reductionist approach can sometimes lead to the misapplication of Stoic principles, where an overemphasis on individual resilience and personal success overshadows the nuances of ethical dilemmas and the importance of community responsibility.

Moreover, the commercialization of Stoicism in the self-help industry raises concerns about the dilution of its philosophical integrity. Stoic principles are often promoted as tools for achieving personal and professional success, but there is a risk that their broader ethical implications may be overlooked. This focus on self-optimization can detract from the communal and philanthropic aspects of Stoic philosophy, which emphasize virtue and moral improvement as ends in themselves, not merely as means to personal gain.

Navigating Modern Stoic Self-Help Literature

As a reader and practitioner of modern Stoicism, it is crucial to engage with these concepts critically, seeking out resources that honor the depth and breadth of Stoic philosophy. By approaching Stoic self-help literature with discernment, you can extract valuable lessons that enhance your life while staying true to Stoicism's ethical and philosophical foundations. This mindful engagement ensures that the wisdom of the Stoics continues to be a source of genuine insight and transformation, rather than merely a commodity in the marketplace of ideas.

12.3 Stoicism and Sustainability: A Philosophical Approach to Environmental Issues

Stoicism's Respect for Nature

At the heart of Stoic philosophy lies a profound respect for nature and an understanding of humanity's place within the natural world. With their emphasis on living in accordance with nature, the Stoics offer a lens through which we can view our environmental responsibilities. They teach us about the interconnectedness of all life and the importance of living in harmony with the world around us. This perspective is not just about appreciating the beauty of nature, but also about recognizing our role as stewards of the earth, with the responsibility to preserve its balance and resources for future generations.

Sympatheia and Environmental Ethics

The Stoic concept of *sympatheia*, or the mutual interdependence of all things, underscores the idea that everything in the universe is connected in a web of existence. From this vantage point, any action impacting the environment reverberates through this network, affecting not just the immediate surroundings but also distant ecosystems and future life. This interconnectedness calls for the practice of temperance—a key Stoic virtue that translates into moderation in the use of natural resources and a mindful approach to consumption. It challenges prevailing attitudes of exploitation and unrestricted consumption, advocating instead for a balance that respects the environment's natural limits and regenerative capacities.

Application of Stoic Principles to Environmental Ethics

Stoic principles such as self-control, moderation, and respect for the natural order provide a robust framework for contemporary environmental ethics. These virtues encourage behaviors that align with sustainable living, prompting individuals to consider the long-term consequences of their actions rather than seeking immediate gratification. For instance, the Stoic practice of self-control can be applied to reduce wasteful consumption. Controlling impulsive buying habits can minimize waste and reduce one's ecological footprint. Similarly, the principle of moderation guides us to consume resources sustainably, ensuring that the earth's bounty is used no faster than it can be replenished.

Respect for Natural Order in Environmental Stewardship

Another Stoic tenet, respect for natural order, inspires a deep reverence for the environment and its intricate systems. This respect fosters practices that protect and preserve natural habitats, support biodiversity, and maintain ecological balance. It encourages policies and personal behaviors that recognize the rights of all beings to exist and thrive, promoting an ethical relationship between humanity and the natural world.

Stoicism in Modern Environmental Movements

Stoic philosophy resonates strongly with the ethos of modern environmental movements, particularly those advocating for minimalist living, zero-waste practices, and systemic change to safeguard the planet. The minimalist lifestyle, for example, is deeply Stoic as it emphasizes simplicity and focuses on the essentials, reducing the clutter of excess possessions and the consequent environmental burden of overconsumption. This lifestyle choice reflects the Stoic ideal of freeing oneself from unnecessary desires and living a life rich in virtue rather than in material wealth.

Zero-Waste Practices and Stoic Resourcefulness

Zero-waste practices align with the Stoic emphasis on resourcefulness and efficiency—principles that encourage waste reduction and the thoughtful use of resources. By adopting habits that minimize waste—such as recycling, composting, and choosing reusable products—individuals embody Stoic virtues by acting responsibly and considerately towards nature.

Moreover, the call for systemic change, a hallmark of many environmental movements, echoes the Stoic commitment to justice and the common good. It recognizes that individual actions, while necessary, are insufficient to address the scale of environmental challenges we face. Systemic change—whether in energy policies, industrial practices, or urban planning—requires a collective shift towards sustainability informed by Stoic principles of fairness, responsibility, and respect for nature.

Case Studies of Stoic-Inspired Environmental Initiatives

Several organizations and communities have explicitly drawn on Stoic principles to shape their environmental policies and practices. One example is a community project in a coastal town that adopted Stoic principles to manage its response to rising sea levels—a direct consequence of climate change. The community implemented a comprehensive plan that included building natural barriers, restoring mangrove forests, and educating residents about sustainable land use practices. This initiative not only helped to mitigate the impact of flooding but also strengthened the community's resilience and cohesiveness by fostering a collective sense of purpose and responsibility.

Another case involves a company that introduced a 'Stoic Sustainability Code' for its operations. The code includes guidelines for reducing energy consumption, managing waste responsibly, and ethically sourcing materials. By integrating Stoic virtues into its operational ethos, the company has improved its environmental impact and set a standard for ethical conduct in the business sector, inspiring other companies to follow suit.

Stoicism's Role in Environmental Stewardship

These examples demonstrate the practical applicability and positive impact of Stoic principles in contemporary environmental efforts. By guiding personal behaviors and informing policy decisions, Stoicism offers enduring insights that are both timely and timeless, urging us to live responsibly as part of a larger, interconnected cosmos.

As we conclude our exploration of Stoicism's role in sustainability and environmental ethics, we are reminded of the power of ancient wisdom in addressing modern challenges. The Stoic call to live virtuously and in harmony with nature is more relevant today than ever, offering guiding principles for environmental stewardship and sustainable living. In the next chapter, we will continue to explore how Stoic philosophy can inform and inspire our approaches to other pressing contemporary issues, reinforcing its relevance and utility in our journey toward a more ethical and sustainable future.

Reflection Questions:

1. What role does spirituality play in Stoic philosophy?
2. How can Stoicism contribute to your spiritual growth and development?
3. In what ways can practicing Stoic virtues lead to a deeper sense of spiritual fulfillment?

Journal Prompts:

1. Reflect on your spiritual beliefs and practices. How can Stoic principles enhance your spiritual journey?
2. Write about a spiritual experience that had a significant impact on you. How can Stoic philosophy help you understand and integrate this experience?
3. Develop a spiritual practice routine based on Stoic principles. What specific actions or reflections will you include to foster spiritual growth?

CHAPTER 13

ADVANCED STOIC THEORIES AND PRACTICES

Imagine navigating a vast ocean, where the waves represent the tumultuous events of your life. Guiding your vessel is your reason, and the compass that directs this reason is the Stoic Logos. In this chapter, we explore the profound depths of the Stoic conception of Logos, a principle that not only offers a map for ethical living but also aligns you with the universe's rational structure.

13.1 The Stoic Conception of Logos and its Implications

Understanding Logos in Stoic Philosophy

Logos in Stoicism can be understood as the rational principle that governs the universe. It's like the rulebook that guides all reason and the force that structures and animates nature. This is not just a fancy idea, but it's as real as the law of gravity, influencing how the cosmos works. The Stoics, who saw the universe as a well-ordered and rational entity, believed that this Logos is everywhere, holding the universe together. Logos works on a grand scale, but it's also at work in each of us, guiding our ability to think and make decisions, which sets us apart from other creatures.

For you, grappling with daily decisions and ethical dilemmas, understanding Logos provides a practical foundation for aligning with this rational order. It suggests that each person, equipped with reason, is part of a larger cosmos, which operates according to its rational laws. This interconnectedness implies that your actions are most harmonious and fulfilling when they align with the rationality of the universe, guided by virtue and wisdom. This practical application of Stoic philosophy empowers you to navigate life's complexities with confidence and capability.

Implications of Logos for Human Behavior

The Stoic belief in Logos implies that you, as part of this rational universe, can recognize and align with its order through your actions and choices. We achieve this alignment through cultivating virtue and practicing rational living. In practical terms, this means that your decisions, when guided by reason and virtue, not only enhance your life but also contribute to the harmony of the universe.

Consider how this plays out in your professional life or personal relationships. Each interaction or decision, when made through the lens of virtue and rationality, resonates with the Logos, promoting individual well-being and the common good. For instance, choosing honesty in your communications fosters trust. It builds stronger relationships, aligning your actions with the Stoic ideal of living according to nature's rational design.

Logos in Ethical Decision-Making

The Stoic understanding of Logos profoundly influences ethical decision-making. It suggests that ethical choices should align with the universe's natural order, which is rational and good. When faced with a decision, you are thus encouraged to consider not just the immediate benefits or consequences but how your choice reflects universal reason.

This approach can transform how you tackle ethical dilemmas, such as those encountered in business or personal ethics. For example, when deciding whether to disclose uncomfortable truths in a business deal, the Stoic, guided by Logos, would choose transparency, as honesty aligns with the rational and harmonious functioning of human interactions.

Contemporary Interpretations of Logos

In modern philosophical and spiritual contexts, the idea of Logos continues to resonate, influencing contemporary discussions about ethics, science, and spirituality. Philosophers and theologians often reference Logos when exploring the intersection of science and religion or debating technological advancements' moral implications. In these discussions, The principle of Logos bridges disparate fields, offering a unifying theory that underscores the compatibility of scientific understanding and ethical reasoning.

For you, living in a world where technological and ethical landscapes are rapidly evolving, the Stoic Logos offers a grounding principle. It encourages you to seek harmony in your actions and beliefs, guided by the rational order that the Stoics believed governs everything. This ancient yet enduring concept serves as a compass, directing your ethical navigation through the complexities of modern life. For instance, when faced with a difficult decision at work, you can use the Stoic Logos to guide your choice, ensuring that it aligns with the rational and harmonious functioning of human interactions.

13.2 Advanced Stoic Practices for Self-Mastery

In pursuing a deeper understanding and application of Stoicism, there comes a point where more than basic exercises may be needed to meet the growing needs of your philosophical and personal development. Advanced Stoic practices come into play at this juncture, designed not only to challenge your existing perceptions but also to foster a level of self-mastery that permeates every aspect of your life. These practices, though demanding, offer profound insights into the nature of your thoughts, emotions, and reactions, guiding you toward greater wisdom and inner strength. They have the potential to transform your life, inspiring you to strive for greater self-mastery and personal development.

The Discipline of Assent

One such advanced practice is the discipline of assent, which focuses on training oneself to give or withhold assent to impressions. In Stoic philosophy, impressions are the initial thoughts or feelings we experience in response to external stimuli, and not all accurately reflect reality. The discipline of assent teaches you to pause and evaluate these impressions, deciding whether they are accurate and whether they should guide your actions. This practice is crucial because it forms the basis of your reactions to every situation.

For example, consider a scenario where you receive unexpected critical feedback at work. Your initial impression might be one of offense or defensiveness, potentially leading to reactive behavior that could exacerbate the situation. Practicing the discipline of assent involves:

- Stepping back from that first impulse.
- Examining the feedback objectively.
- Deciding whether it is a justified critique that can aid your professional growth.

By assenting to the feedback's constructive elements and discarding any unhelpful emotional reactions, you maintain your composure and turn a potentially harmful experience into a valuable learning opportunity.

Implementing this practice requires consistent effort. It begins with mindfulness of your automatic thoughts and emotions, observing them without immediate reaction. Over time, this awareness builds a mental space where you can assess and control your impressions before solidifying into beliefs or actions. This aspect of Stoic practice enhances your emotional intelligence. It empowers you to live more deliberately, making choices that align with your values and the greater good.

Role-Playing Exercises for Moral Imagination

Another profound technique to deepen your Stoic practice is engaging in role-playing exercises that enhance your moral imagination. These exercises involve envisioning yourself in various challenging moral scenarios to test and strengthen your virtues and decision-making capabilities under pressure. By simulating complex ethical dilemmas or personal trials, you can explore different responses and their consequences in a controlled, reflective manner.

For instance, you might imagine a situation where you must choose between two conflicting duties: your responsibility to your family and your obligations at work. Consider how different choices would align with Stoic virtues such as duty, justice, and temperance in this imagined scenario. Reflect on the potential impacts of each decision, not just immediately but also in the long term. This exercise sharpens your ethical reasoning and prepares you for real-life situations where similar dilemmas might arise, enabling you to act with integrity and wisdom.

Integration of Stoic Practices into Daily Rituals

Integration into your daily life is essential to benefit from these advanced Stoic practices. Setting aside regular time for practices like the discipline of assent and role-playing moral scenarios as part of your daily or weekly routines is essential. Morning is often ideal for such reflections, as it sets a thoughtful tone for the day ahead. Alternatively, evening reflection allows one to assess the day's events and your responses, enabling continuous learning and improvement.

Incorporating these practices into your life involves:

- Creating physical or digital reminders of Stoic principles.
- Keep a journal of your reflections and progress.
- Forming a discussion group with others interested in Stoicism.

These actions help maintain your commitment to Stoic discipline and ensure that its principles deeply influence your way of being, transforming your actions and character.

Engaging with these advanced Stoic practices opens you to a higher level of philosophical insight and personal growth. This journey towards self-mastery is not always easy, but it is profoundly rewarding. It offers you the tools to live with greater purpose, resilience, and harmony both within yourself and in relation to the world around you. Through diligent practice and reflection, you cultivate a life that is not only reactive to external circumstances but actively shaped by your highest values and reasoned choices.

13.3 The Stoic's Guide to Achieving Ataraxia (Tranquility)

Defining Ataraxia

Ataraxia, often translated as tranquility or imperturbability, is the ultimate goal of Stoic practice. In this state, one achieves profound serenity, remaining unaffected by external turmoil or internal storms of passion. This sublime state of being is not merely about the absence of disturbance; rather, it embodies a deep, enduring peace that comes from living in harmony with reason and virtue.

The Path to Ataraxia

Understanding and pursuing Ataraxia involves a philosophical journey that is both challenging and rewarding. The Stoics believed that achieving this state is possible through living in accordance with nature, which includes aligning one's beliefs and actions with the rational order of the universe. This alignment is not passive; it requires active engagement with your thoughts and decisions, ensuring that wisdom and virtue govern them.

Rigorous Examination and Alignment

The process of aligning oneself with Stoic principles involves a rigorous examination of one's beliefs, systematically discarding those that lead to irrational passions or disturbances, and cultivating those that enhance one's rational understanding of the world. This careful and continuous self-assessment is central to progressing toward Ataraxia.

Practices for Cultivating Calm and Resilience

Practices designed to cultivate an inner landscape of calm and resilience pave the path to Ataraxia. Regular meditation on one's thoughts and actions is a foundational practice. This involves reflectively examining the start or end of each day, assessing whether your actions aligned with Stoic virtues and whether your responses to external events were guided by reason rather than impulse. Through such meditative introspection, you gain insights into your behavioral patterns and develop the ability to modulate your responses in alignment with Stoic teachings.

Detachment from Desires and Aversions

Another crucial practice is cultivating detachment from desires and aversions. In Stoic terms, this involves understanding that while preferences for specific outcomes are natural, the peace of your inner state should not be contingent on these outcomes. Practicing detachment means training yourself to accept different outcomes with equanimity, whether they align with your preferences or not. This doesn't mean adopting a passive or indifferent attitude towards life's events; instead, it's about embracing a proactive tranquility that remains steady regardless of circumstances.

Mindfulness in Response to External Events

Moreover, practicing mindfulness in response to external events is vital. This form of mindfulness goes beyond merely being present in the moment. It requires you to consciously know how you process external events through your Stoic beliefs. It's about observing how impressions form in your mind and choosing to respond with actions that reflect the Stoic virtues of wisdom, justice, courage, and moderation.

Challenges in the Pursuit of Ataraxia

Despite its profound benefits, the pursuit of Ataraxia is challenging. It demands steadfast dedication to philosophical practice and often requires confronting and modifying deeply ingrained habits. The societal pressure to conform to norms that do not align with Stoic principles can pose significant challenges. However, the rewards of pursuing Ataraxia are immense. Achieving this state of Stoic tranquility brings personal peace and a resilient disposition that can weather life's vicissitudes with grace and fortitude.

A Dynamic and Ongoing Process

As you integrate these practices into your life, remember that pursuing Ataraxia is not a static goal but a dynamic process of continual growth and understanding. It is about cultivating a state of being that reflects the highest potentials of human nature, guided by reason and enriched by virtue. Once achieved, this tranquil state not only enhances your own life but also allows you to contribute to the world with greater clarity and purpose.

In wrapping up this exploration of Ataraxia, the journey through Stoic practices offers a transformative path to personal tranquility and a deeper engagement with the world. In the next chapter, we will actively explore how to apply these Stoic principles to foster robust, enriching relationships, enhance individual lives, and strengthen the fabric of our communities.

Reflection Questions:

1. How does Stoicism view the concept of legacy and lasting impact?
2. What actions can you take to ensure that your legacy reflects Stoic virtues?
3. How can you inspire others to practice Stoicism through your example?

Journal Prompts:

1. Reflect on the legacy you want to leave behind. How can Stoic principles guide you in creating this legacy?
2. Write about a person whose legacy you admire. How did they embody Stoic virtues, and how can you emulate their example?
3. Create a plan for how you will live each day with the intention of leaving a positive legacy. What specific actions will you take to ensure your legacy reflects Stoic virtues?

CHAPTER 14

STOICISM FOR LIFE'S PEAKS AND VALLEYS

As we navigate the undulating terrain of life's successes and setbacks, the Stoic philosophy offers a compass that steadies our stride regardless of the ground beneath us. This chapter turns its focus to a counterintuitive yet profound aspect of Stoicism: the art of embracing success with humility. While modern culture often exalts success as an ultimate aim, Stoicism invites us to view it differently—not as an endpoint but as a path that can be walked with wisdom, virtue, and humility.

14.1 Embracing Success with Humility: A Stoic Approach

Understanding the Stoic View on Success

In Stoicism, success is not just an endpoint but a 'preferred indifferent'—it is preferred because it can facilitate a life of virtue. This nuanced view challenges the conventional glorification of success. Stoics argue that while achieving goals can be beneficial, the ethical manner in which we attain and handle these achievements is paramount. Thus, success, when it arrives, should be welcomed with the same equanimity as when it eludes us. This perspective ensures that one's happiness is not contingent on external accolades or achievements but on maintaining integrity and virtue.

Practical Advice for Handling Success

The Stoic approach to managing success involves consciously maintaining humility and perspective, which in turn keeps us grounded and balanced. Here are some strategies you might consider:

Reflect on the Impermanence of Success: Just as the Stoics contemplate the transitory nature of life's hardships, they also advise reflecting on the ephemeral (short-lived) nature of success. This practice helps temper the intoxication of achievements with the sobering reminder that every peak is paired with a valley. Such reflection not only grounds you but also prepares you for future fluctuations in fortune.

Acknowledge the Contributions of Others: No success is a solo feat. Recognizing the efforts of those who supported you—be it through direct collaboration or indirect influence—fosters humility and gratitude. This practice enhances interpersonal relationships and dilutes any burgeoning egoism that success might ferment.

Engage in Regular Self-Reflection: Stoicism encourages continual self-assessment to ensure that one's actions remain aligned with personal values and virtues. After achieving success, take time to reflect on how you have changed, how you handled the process, and how you can improve further. This reflective practice is crucial in keeping your feet firmly planted on the ground, even as you reach for the stars.

The Crucial Role of Self-Awareness in Navigating Success

Practicing self-awareness involves regularly checking in with oneself and inviting feedback from others whose opinions you trust. This could be through formal mechanisms like performance reviews or informal conversations with friends and mentors. The feedback received should be contemplated, not defensively, allowing you to view yourself from an external perspective and identify areas for improvement.

Applying Stoicism in Real-Life Situations

To further understand how Stoicism can be applied to embrace success with humility in real-life situations, consider the following practices:

Focus on Virtue, Not Outcomes: Stoics believe true success lies in living virtuously, not external achievements. When you achieve success, remember that it results from your virtues—wisdom, courage, and perseverance. By focusing on these inner qualities rather than the external outcomes, you can maintain humility and avoid becoming overly attached to the recognition or rewards that come with success.

Practice Gratitude and Acknowledgment of Others: Acknowledge that your success is often a result of contributions from others, whether it's colleagues, mentors, or even circumstances beyond your control. Expressing gratitude keeps you grounded and helps you find joy in the ordinary, preventing pride from overshadowing your achievements.

Reflect on the Transience of Success: Recognize that success, like all things in life, is ephemeral. What is celebrated today may be forgotten tomorrow. This awareness helps keep your ego in check and encourages you to continue striving for excellence without becoming complacent or arrogant.

Use Success as an Opportunity to Serve Others: A fundamental Stoic principle is the common good. Use your success as a platform to help others by mentoring, sharing knowledge, or contributing to your community. This reinforces the idea that success is not solely for personal gain but also the benefit of others.

Engage in Regular Self-Reflection: Continuously reflect on your actions and decisions, asking yourself whether they align with Stoic virtues. This practice helps you maintain perspective and humility, ensuring your success does not lead to hubris.

By applying these Stoic principles, you can embrace success with humility, recognizing it as a step in your ongoing journey of personal growth and virtuous living rather than an endpoint or source of self-importance.

Examples from Stoic Figures

Historical Stoic figures provide rich examples of handling success with humility. Consider Seneca, a man of considerable wealth and political power, who frequently wrote about the dangers of success leading to hubris. His letters and essays serve as reminders of the importance of grounding success in virtue and wisdom. Similarly, Marcus Aurelius, despite being one of the most powerful men in the world as the Roman Emperor, journaled daily reminders to himself about the importance of humility, service, and the common good.

These Stoic thinkers reached great heights while staying acutely aware of the fleeting nature of success and the enduring importance of virtue. Their lives and writings illustrate that success, when infused with Stoic principles, can elevate oneself and those around us, creating a legacy that outlives the ephemeral glow of worldly achievements.

As you reflect on these teachings and the stories of those who walked before you, consider how you might integrate Stoic humility into your peaks of success. In doing so, you enhance your capacity to handle success gracefully and deepen your engagement with the core Stoic pursuit of a virtuous life. Embracing success with humility is not about diminishing your achievements but elevating your response to them, ensuring that they contribute to a well-lived life of Stoic virtue.

14.2 Stoic Resilience in the Face of Failure

The Stoic Perspective on Failure

In the Stoic view, failure, much like success, is perceived as an external event that does not fundamentally define us or our moral values. Similarly, success is not seen as a measure of our worth, but as a byproduct of our actions and virtues. This perspective is crucial, particularly in a society that often equates success with personal merit. Stoicism teaches us to see both success and failure as natural parts of the human experience, inevitable companions on the path to achievement and wisdom.

More critically, failure is a fertile ground for growth and learning. Embracing this view transforms the sting of failure into an invitation to fortify one's character and skills, empowering us with the knowledge that we can learn and grow from every setback. This transformative power of Stoic resilience not only helps us recover from failure but positions it as a stepping stone toward greater understanding and capability.

Redefining Failure as an Opportunity for Growth

In the Stoic framework, failure is not a terminal verdict but a valuable teacher. When we redefine failure as an opportunity for growth, we shift our mindset from despair to curiosity and determination. Instead of seeing failure as a reflection of our inadequacies, we begin to view it as a natural part of the learning process, an essential component of progress. This perspective encourages us to embrace challenges with a mindset that is not afraid of mistakes but rather eager to learn from them. This shift in perception is vital in fostering resilience, as it empowers us to face difficulties with the confidence that each setback brings us closer to wisdom and improvement.

Stoics believe that every obstacle is an opportunity to practice virtue. In the face of failure, virtues such as courage, patience, and humility come to the forefront. Courage is required to face the reality of the setback without denial; patience is necessary to endure the discomfort of the situation and the time it might take to recover. Humility allows us to accept our limitations and learn from the experience. By practicing these virtues, we recover from failure and grow stronger in character.

Practical Stoic Exercises for Learning from Failure

Stoic philosophy offers a variety of practical exercises that encourage us to reflect on our failures—not to dwell on them with regret, but to analyze them to garner wisdom. These exercises are theoretical concepts and practical tools that equip us to learn and grow from our failures. One such practice involves a structured reflection where you recount a recent failure and methodically dissect it to understand what went wrong, why it went wrong, and how similar pitfalls can be avoided. Another exercise could be the 'view from above ', where you imagine yourself from a distance, observing the situation objectively. This exercise is not about assigning blame but about extracting actionable insights that can lead to better future outcomes.

For instance, if a work project did not meet its objectives, instead of marinating in frustration or disappointment, a Stoic would assess the planning and execution stages. Were unrealistic deadlines set? Did communication falter? Were resources allocated effectively? By breaking down each process component, you can identify specific areas for improvement. This practice of systematic reflection helps prevent future failures. It builds a proactive approach to problem-solving grounded in reason and self-awareness, instilling in us a sense of confidence and preparedness for future challenges.

Another valuable Stoic exercise is journaling. By keeping a daily or weekly journal in which you reflect on your successes and failures, you create a space for continuous self-improvement. Writing about your experiences allows you to process emotions, clarify your thoughts, and develop a deeper understanding of the patterns that lead to success or failure. Over time, this practice enhances your ability to respond to setbacks with resilience and wisdom.

Developing Mental Resilience Through Premeditation of Adversity

One of the key Stoic practices in building resilience against failure is *Premeditatio Malorum* or the premeditation of adversity. Mentally preparing for potential setbacks before they occur is essential. By imagining scenarios where things could go wrong, you train your mind to stay calm and composed when facing real challenges. This practice helps reduce the shock and emotional turmoil often accompanying failure, as you have already rehearsed your response to adversity.

For example, before starting a new venture, you might contemplate the possibility of financial loss, rejection, or unforeseen obstacles. Doing so creates a mental buffer that allows you to handle these situations more rationally and less emotionally if they arise. This doesn't mean expecting the worst at all times but being mentally prepared to face challenges without losing your composure.

Maintaining Equanimity in the Face of Setbacks

Maintaining equanimity in the face of setbacks is a hallmark of Stoic resilience. Stoicism teaches that our initial emotional reactions to failure are natural. Yet, they must not govern our actions or cloud our judgment. The Stoics understood that emotions like disappointment, frustration, or even anger are common responses to failure. Still, they also recognized the importance of not letting these emotions dictate our behavior.

Techniques such as deep breathing, pausing to reflect before responding, and speaking about the failure objectively can help manage these emotional responses. For example, when faced with a setback, instead of reacting impulsively, a Stoic would take a moment to breathe deeply, center themselves, and then approach the situation with a calm, rational mindset. Creating a mental space between the event and your response is crucial for maintaining composure and making thoughtful decisions.

By reframing setbacks as neutral events—opportunities for learning and growth rather than catastrophes—we can preserve our mental tranquility and remain open to the lessons they offer. This approach minimizes the emotional toll of failure and enhances our ability to learn and adapt. The Stoic practice of maintaining equanimity helps us stay grounded, even in the face of adversity, allowing us to move forward with clarity and purpose.

Examples of Stoic Resilience in Action

The power of Stoic resilience is not just theoretical; it can be observed in the lives of historical and contemporary figures who embody these principles. Consider the story of Thomas Edison, whose ventures failed thousands of times before he successfully invented the light bulb. Edison's response to his many setbacks is a testament to Stoic resilience. He famously reframed his failures by saying, "I have not failed. I've just found 10,000 ways that won't work." This perspective exemplifies the Stoic belief that failure is a part of innovation and discovery. By maintaining a positive outlook and learning from each attempt, Edison achieved one of history's most significant technological breakthroughs.

Another poignant example is J.K. Rowling, who faced numerous rejections from publishers but persisted with her vision, eventually leading to the creation of the Harry Potter series, a global literary phenomenon. Rowling's journey from struggling writer to international success highlights the importance of resilience, perseverance, and staying true to one's values and goals. Her story underscores a core Stoic belief: resilience is not inherent but cultivated through persistent effort and the rational appraisal of obstacles. By embracing failure as a necessary step toward success, Rowling exemplifies the Stoic attitude of turning adversity into opportunity.

Drawing Inspiration from Epictetus

Epictetus, born into slavery and later became one of the most influential Stoic philosophers, offers a profound example of resilience in the face of adversity. Despite his harsh circumstances, Epictetus taught that we have control over our attitudes and responses to external events, even when we cannot control those events. His famous quote, *"It's not what happens to you, but how you react to it that matters,"* encapsulates the Stoic approach to failure.

Epictetus emphasized the importance of focusing on what we can control—our thoughts, beliefs, and actions—while accepting what we cannot. This teaching is particularly relevant when dealing with failure, as it reminds us to direct our energy towards constructive actions and let go of the desire to control outcomes beyond our reach. By internalizing this wisdom, we can navigate failures with a calm mind and a resilient spirit, transforming setbacks into opportunities for personal growth.

Developing Robustness Through Stoic Practices

Integrating these Stoic practices into our lives helps us develop a robustness that stands firm through life's vicissitudes. This resilience enables us to approach failure not with fear or aversion but with confidence and a readiness to extract wisdom from every experience. As you encounter your failures, large or small, remember that each is not a verdict on your capabilities but a call to action—a challenge to rise, learn, and expand your horizons.

Through this lens, every failure contributes to sculpting a wiser, more competent self fully engaged in the lifelong pursuit of virtue and excellence.

The journey of personal growth, guided by Stoic principles, is one where setbacks are seen not as defeats but as opportunities for refinement and improvement. By embracing this mindset, you cultivate a resilience that helps you overcome challenges and transforms them into stepping stones on your path to a more virtuous and fulfilling life.

The Importance of Community and Support in Resilience

While Stoicism emphasizes individual resilience, it also recognizes the value of community and support in navigating failure. Surrounding yourself with like-minded individuals who share your commitment to growth and virtue can provide invaluable encouragement and perspective during difficult times. Whether through formal Stoic study groups, mentorship relationships, or simply supportive friendships, these connections can help you stay motivated and grounded as you work through setbacks.

Sharing your experiences and learning from others' stories of resilience can further strengthen your resolve and remind you that you are not alone in your struggles. The Stoic community, whether historical or contemporary, offers a wealth of wisdom and solidarity that can guide you through the most challenging periods of your life.

Reflecting on the Nature of Success and Failure

Stoic philosophy teaches that success and failure are not absolute opposites but are part of a continuous cycle of growth and learning. By reflecting on the transient nature of both, we can gain a deeper understanding of their true significance in our lives. Success should be approached with humility and an awareness of its impermanence. At the same time, failure should be met with resilience and a willingness to learn. This balanced approach helps us maintain a steady course through life's highs and lows, grounded in the principles of virtue and wisdom.

Final Thoughts on Stoic Resilience

As you integrate Stoic practices into your daily life, remember that resilience is a skill that develops over time. Through repeated practice, reflection, and perseverance, you build the inner strength needed to face life's challenges with grace and fortitude. By embracing failure as a teacher and using it to refine your character, you overcome obstacles and pave the way for more profound personal growth and fulfillment. The Stoic path is one of continuous improvement, where each setback is an opportunity to cultivate the virtues that lead to a life of wisdom, courage, and enduring peace.

14.3 Finding Joy in the Ordinary: Stoic Lessons on Gratitude and Presence

In the simplicity of daily life, where routine can overshadow novelty, Stoicism finds a treasure trove of joy and serenity. This philosophy does not chase after the extraordinary; instead, it cultivates a deep appreciation for the ordinary moments that fabricate our everyday existence. Stoics understand that life's value often lies not in rare peak experiences but in the quiet moments we frequently overlook—the morning sunlight through the window, a shared laugh during a family meal, or the peaceful silence at day's end. These instances hold the essence of Stoic joy: a profound appreciation for what is rather than a longing for what could be.

Mindfulness and present-moment awareness are essential Stoic practices that enhance this appreciation. By being fully present, we engage directly with life as it unfolds, without the distractions of past regrets or future anxieties. This focus on the present not only heightens our experience of everyday joys but also shifts our perspective from lack to abundance. To practice this, consider the simple act of a meditative walk—where instead of the usual pace and preoccupation with thoughts, you slow down and notice the sensations around you, the feel of the breeze, the sounds of the birds, or the patterns of the leaves. Such mindfulness deepens your connection with the environment and cultivates a grounded feeling of contentment.

Gratitude is another powerful Stoic tool that transforms our perception of daily life. It shifts our focus from what we lack to the abundance surrounding us. Stoicism teaches us to be grateful for the good and the challenges, as each difficulty carries a lesson or strength to be gained. To integrate gratitude into daily life, start by maintaining a gratitude journal. Each night, jot down three things you were grateful for that day. These need not be grand events; the most profound gratitude often arises from appreciating the mundane—a warm home, a kind word from a stranger, or the comfort of your favorite chair. Over time, this practice can shift your baseline of happiness higher, making joy a more constant companion.

The benefits of embracing Stoic lessons on gratitude and presence are manifold. Psychologically, this approach helps in reducing anxiety and depression by anchoring you in the positive aspects of your current experience. Emotionally, it fosters a more profound satisfaction with life, as you no longer perpetually reach for the next big thing to make you happy. Socially, it enriches your relationships, as gratitude and mindfulness increase your empathy and attentiveness towards others, strengthening connections and fostering mutual appreciation.

As you engage more deeply with these Stoic practices, the ordinary becomes extraordinary. The daily coffee is no longer just a routine; it becomes a ritual of comfort and awakening. Conversations with loved ones grow richer as you become more present and engaged. Even challenges can be seen through gratitude, recognized as opportunities for growth and learning. Through this Stoic lens, life becomes a series of moments to be savored, each holding potential for joy and discovery.

As this chapter closes, reflect on how the simple practices of mindfulness and gratitude can profoundly transform your daily experience. By finding joy in the ordinary and embracing each moment with presence, you cultivate a life not just lived but fully experienced. This approach enriches your journey and inspires those around you, spreading a quiet yet powerful ripple of contentment and appreciation through the fabric of everyday life. As we transition to the next chapter, carry forward this sense of gratitude and presence, exploring how they can continue to enhance your resilience, relationships, and engagements with the world around you.

CHAPTER 15

PRACTICAL EXAMPLES OF STOIC DECISION MAKING

Our decisions are pivotal in the intricate dance of life, where each step forward can alter our journey. Stoicism, with its profound emphasis on virtue and reason, offers a compass for navigating these decisions, ensuring they lead us through life and towards a more meaningful existence. This chapter delves into how Stoic principles guide us in making decisions that resonate deeply with our values, enhance our well-being, and maintain harmony in our relationships, all while facing professional challenges with integrity and wisdom.

15.1 Personal Life Decisions

Career Choices: Aligning Ambition with Integrity

Imagine standing at a crossroads in your career where one direction offers a lucrative job laden with ethical compromises and the other a less financially rewarding role aligned with your core values and principles—this scenario, common in the professional landscape, tests our ambitions and integrity. A Stoic, guided by the pursuit of virtue rather than external rewards, approaches this decision with a focus on long-term fulfillment and ethical consistency.

Consider the case of John, a talented software developer offered a high-paying position in a company known for its aggressive, profit-driven strategies that often skirt legal boundaries. The alternative is a modestly paying job in a nonprofit organization dedicated to educational equity—an issue close to John's heart. Through a Stoic lens, this decision transcends financial gain. It involves considering which role allows John to live by his virtues, such as integrity and justice, and which job will contribute positively to his growth as a virtuous individual. Stoicism empowers John to reflect on the kind of person he wants to be and the societal impact of his work, guiding him to choose the path that strengthens his character and serves the common good rather than merely enhancing his wealth.

Exercise: Reflecting on Career Choices

Take a moment to reflect on a significant career decision you've made or are currently facing. Write down the options before you and list the virtues associated with each choice. Ask yourself:

- Which option aligns most closely with your core values?
- How will this decision impact your long-term fulfillment and growth as a virtuous individual?
- Are there any ethical compromises involved? How do they weigh against the potential benefits?

Use this reflection to guide your decision-making process, ensuring that your choices align with your values and contribute to your personal growth.

Health and Lifestyle: Cultivating Discipline for Well-Being

Stoicism teaches discipline and rationality, virtues that are particularly relevant when making decisions about health and lifestyle. The Stoic view is not austerity but choosing a lifestyle that maintains the body and mind in its best state, supporting one's ability to live virtuously. For instance, let's consider Mia, who struggles with maintaining a healthy lifestyle amidst a demanding career. Due to her busy schedule, sedentary habits and convenience foods have become the norm. However, by embracing Stoicism, Mia gains a clear understanding of her health as essential to her moral duty to care for herself and, by extension, her ability to care for others.

She understands that discipline in exercise and dietary habits isn't a punishment but a rational choice to enhance her well-being and longevity. By applying Stoic principles, Mia starts planning her meals and scheduling regular physical activities, viewing these actions not as chores but as parts of a virtuous life that respects her body's natural needs. Over time, Mia discovers that this disciplined approach improves her health and mental clarity, making her more effective in her work and personal life.

Exercise: Planning a Stoic Lifestyle

Create a weekly plan that includes time for physical exercise, meal planning, and mental relaxation. Reflect on how each activity supports your overall well-being and ability to live according to Stoic virtues.

Consider:

- How can you make healthier choices that align with Stoic principles of discipline and rationality?
- What small changes can you implement to maintain this lifestyle consistently?

Monitor your progress and adjust your plan, ensuring your lifestyle supports your physical and mental well-being.

Conflict Resolution: Fostering Harmony Through Understanding

Conflicts are inevitable in relationships, but their resolution doesn't have to disrupt harmony if approached with Stoicism. The Stoic method emphasizes understanding, controlling emotional reactions, and seeking resolutions that restore and maintain the relationship's integrity. Imagine Leo and Jamie, who share a close friendship but are in a heated disagreement over a business venture. Instead of allowing anger to dictate his responses, Leo applies Stoic principles. He strives to understand Jamie's perspective fully, acknowledging his friend's concerns without immediate judgment or defensive reactions.

By focusing on empathetic listening and keeping his emotions in check, Leo finds a pathway to propose a compromise that aligns with their interests, thus preserving the strength and integrity of their friendship. This approach not only resolves the conflict but also strengthens their bond, demonstrating the power of Stoicism in maintaining relationships and bringing a sense of peace and harmony.

Exercise: Practicing Stoic Conflict Resolution

Think about a recent conflict you've experienced. Reflect on how you responded and could have applied Stoic principles to handle the situation more effectively. Consider:

- How did your emotions influence your reactions?
- What could you have done to understand the other person's perspective better?
- How might you approach similar conflicts in the future with a Stoic mindset?

Write down your reflections and use them as a guide for resolving future conflicts with empathy and rationality.

Relationship Choices: Prioritizing Well-Being and Virtue

Stoicism also guides the decision-making process in complex personal relationships. It teaches that maintaining a toxic relationship contradicts Stoic virtues, such as self-respect and rational self-care. Consider Sarah, who finds herself in a partnership that has grown increasingly detrimental to her well-being. Stoicism would counsel Sarah to prioritize her mental health and personal growth. It would encourage her to view the relationship objectively, recognizing that genuine affection and companionship should not be sources of continual distress.

Guided by Stoicism, Sarah makes the painful but rational decision to end the relationship. This choice aligns with Stoic principles of protecting her well-being and living free from emotional turmoil. While challenging, this decision ultimately leads Sarah to a path of healing and self-discovery, allowing her to rebuild her life in a way that aligns more closely with her values.

Exercise: Evaluating Relationships through Stoic Principles

Reflect on your current relationships—whether romantic, familial, or friendships. Ask yourself:

- Are these relationships enhancing your well-being and supporting your growth?
- Do they align with Stoic virtues such as respect, integrity, and mutual support?
- If there are challenges, how can you address them in a way that maintains your well-being and aligns with Stoic principles?

Use this reflection to make informed decisions about nurturing or adjusting these relationships for the better.

Professional Decisions: Overcoming Challenges in Decision-Making

Navigating Ethical Dilemmas with Integrity

Navigating professional challenges with Stoic principles involves a commitment to integrity and rational problem-solving. In the corporate world, decisions often have significant consequences for many individuals, making the Stoic commitment to rational and ethical decision-making not just a personal virtue but a professional necessity. This approach becomes particularly relevant in scenarios involving ethical dilemmas when the right course of action is determined not by profit but by a commitment to justice and the common good.

Consider a scenario involving Elena, a corporate executive who either cuts costs by downsizing her team, potentially putting several employees out of work, or finding alternative solutions that might reduce immediate profits but preserve her team's jobs. A Stoic approach would guide Elena in evaluating the situation not just through a financial lens but with a focus on virtue and the welfare of her team.

By valuing human dignity and the impact of her decisions on others' lives, Elena explores creative solutions that uphold the company's financial health without compromising her ethical responsibilities. Her decision-making process, informed by Stoicism, reflects a balance of courage, justice, and practical wisdom, ensuring her actions contribute positively to her company and her team.

Exercise: Applying Stoic Principles to Professional Dilemmas

Think about a challenging decision you've faced or are currently facing professionally. Reflect on how you can apply Stoic principles to guide your decision-making process.

Consider:

- What are the potential ethical implications of each option?
- How can you prioritize the well-being of others while maintaining professional integrity?
- What creative solutions might exist that align with Stoic virtues and still address the challenge at hand?

Document your reflections and use them to guide your actions in the workplace, ensuring that your decisions reflect a commitment to ethical and rational principles.

In each of these scenarios, Stoicism doesn't merely offer a way to make decisions; it provides a framework for making decisions that enrich our lives and align with our deepest values. Through the lens of Stoicism, we see not just the choices before us but the kind of individuals we aspire to be—rational, virtuous, and deeply engaged in pursuing a meaningful life.

15.2 The Stoic Commitment to Rational Decision-Making

The Foundation of Stoic Rationality

In our exploration of Stoicism, we recognize that the essence of Stoic decision-making is not merely about making choices that serve immediate needs or personal desires but about fostering a deeper adherence to rationality and virtue. This commitment is foundational, guiding individuals through the complexities of both personal and professional life with a steadfast moral compass. Stoicism does not offer a retreat from the world's challenges but equips us to engage with them more profoundly and ethically.

The Process of Rational Decision-Making

Rational decision-making in Stoicism involves a thorough process where each choice is evaluated based on its alignment with virtue. It's about asking, "Does this decision enhance my character? Does it contribute positively to the community?" This approach is based on the Stoic belief that genuine happiness comes from virtue and that every decision is an opportunity to uphold or undermine this principle.

Reflecting on various scenarios we've navigated, whether choosing careers that resonate with our deepest values or resolving conflicts with empathy and perspective-taking, the role of rationality has been unmistakable. Each instance underscores the transformational power of decisions made through the lens of Stoic rationality.

Continuous Application and Growth

To consistently apply these principles, it is essential to recognize that Stoicism is not a static philosophy but a practice that evolves with each decision we make. It requires vigilance and commitment to align our choices with Stoic virtues continually. This practice is not about perfection but progress; it is a journey towards becoming better individuals and contributing to a more rational and virtuous society.

By responding to life's challenges with reason and integrity, we gradually reinforce a pattern of thinking and behavior that leads to personal growth and profoundly impacts those around us.

Reflecting on Stoic Decision-Making

Reflecting on the adoption of Stoic decision-making, it's clear that this is not merely a philosophical exercise but a practical approach to living a fulfilled and ethical life. Stoicism encourages us not only to think but to act consistently with our highest ideals. It teaches us that every decision, no matter how small, impacts our character and, by extension, the world.

This realization is empowering and daunting, urging us to live deliberately, with mindfulness of how our actions resonate beyond our immediate surroundings.

Exercise: Daily Reflection on Decision-Making

End each day with a brief reflection on the decisions you made. Ask yourself:

- Did my choices align with Stoic virtues?
- How did I handle challenges and dilemmas? Could I have applied Stoic principles more effectively?
- What can I learn from today's decisions that will help me grow?

Use these reflections to continually refine your decision-making process, ensuring that each choice brings you closer to living a life guided by virtue and reason.

As we conclude this discussion on Stoic decision-making, it's evident that the principles of Stoicism offer more than just a methodology for navigating life's practicalities; they provide a framework for a life well-lived. Each decision, viewed through the lens of Stoicism, is a step towards a more rational, virtuous existence, profoundly impacting personal growth and societal well-being.

In the next chapter, we will explore how these principles apply specifically to emotional resilience, further demonstrating the practicality and depth of Stoic philosophy in enhancing our ability to cope with and thrive amidst life's inevitable challenges.

Reflection Questions:

1. How does Stoicism encourage a responsible and respectful relationship with the environment?

2. What actions can you take to align your lifestyle with Stoic principles of environmental stewardship?
3. How can practicing Stoic virtues contribute to a more sustainable and ethical approach to environmental issues?

Journal Prompts:

1. Reflect on your current environmental practices. How can Stoic principles guide you in making more sustainable choices?
2. Write about an environmental issue that concerns you. How can Stoic practices help you contribute to solutions for this issue?
3. Create a plan to incorporate Stoic principles into your daily environmental practices. What specific actions will you take to reduce your ecological footprint and promote sustainability?

CHAPTER 16

STOICISM AND MODERN TECHNOLOGY

In an era where digital landscapes continually reshape the fabric of our daily lives, the ancient philosophy of Stoicism provides a sanctuary of wisdom and practical strategies for navigating this ever-evolving world. As we delve into the intersection of Stoic principles and modern technology, consider how these timeless insights can help us manage the digital tools and information that empower and overwhelm us.

16.1 Stoic Principles in the Digital Age

Adapting Stoicism to Modern Technology

As you navigate the whirlwind of technological advancements, you must anchor your digital interactions in Stoic virtues, particularly moderation, mindfulness, and integrity. Stoicism teaches us to use external goods to practice virtue rather than as ends in themselves. This perspective is crucial when approaching platforms like social media, which, while offering means of connection and knowledge, often encourage excess and distraction.

Moderation in digital consumption is akin to the Stoic practice of temperance, which advocates for balance in all aspects of life. For you, this might mean setting specific boundaries for social media use—perhaps limiting checks to once every few hours rather than minutes. This prevents habitual scrolling, which can consume much of our day, and frees up time for more meaningful activities that align with your values, such as reading, meditating, or spending time with loved ones.

Mindful consumption is another Stoic principle that can transform your interaction with technology. By being selective about the content you engage with online, you ensure that what you consume contributes positively to your well-being and growth. Choose to follow feeds that inspire and educate rather than those that stir envy or discontent. In doing so, you practice the Stoic ideal of focusing on what improves your character and understanding of the world.

Maintaining personal virtue and integrity online is the most critical application of Stoicism in the digital age. In a realm where anonymity can encourage negative behavior, choose to be genuine and kind in all your online interactions, reflecting the Stoic belief in the inherent worth of every individual. Whether it's a tweet, a comment on a blog, or a message on a forum, let your words be guided by Stoic wisdom—tempered with reason and empathy.

Managing Information Overload

The deluge of information that digital technology ushers into daily life can often lead to being overwhelmed and distracted. Here, the Stoic emphasis on simplicity and focus provides a valuable framework. To manage information overload, consider implementing digital detoxes—designated times when you disconnect from all digital devices to reconnect with yourself and your environment. This practice reduces stress and helps cultivate the Stoic virtue of self-sufficiency, reminding you that your peace and contentment come from within, not from the incessant notifications of the digital world.

Furthermore, prioritize information that is meaningful and beneficial. This can be achieved by curating your news feeds and subscriptions to include reputable sources that align with your personal and professional development goals. By doing so, you exercise the Stoic discipline of assent, accepting only the information that serves your growth and dismissing that which causes distraction or distress.

Maintaining Privacy and Integrity

In an online world brimming with data breaches and misinformation, protecting your privacy and navigating interactions with integrity are paramount. Stoicism, with its core values of wisdom and justice, encourages a thoughtful approach to privacy. Be discerning about the personal information you share online, understanding the potential long-term implications of your digital footprint. Just as Stoics reflect on their actions and impact on their character and life, reflect on how your digital behaviors affect your privacy and integrity.

Moreover, interact online with the authenticity and honesty you strive for in face-to-face interactions. Avoid the facade of perfection often portrayed on social media platforms and choose instead to share your true self, with all its virtues and vulnerabilities. This authenticity fosters genuine connections and strengthens your character as you align your digital persona with your Stoic values.

Navigating the complexities of modern technology through a Stoic lens invites you to use digital tools more wisely and ethically and transform your interactions with technology into opportunities for practicing virtue. By applying moderation, mindfulness, and integrity to your digital life, you uphold the Stoic ideal of living harmoniously within the bounds of reason and virtue, no matter the external circumstances.

16.2 Stoic Mindfulness and Digital Distractions

Cultivating Mindfulness Amidst Digital Noise

In an era where the digital hum is as constant as the flow of time, maintaining a laser focus on what truly matters can sometimes seem impossible. The Stoic practice of mindfulness, deeply embedded in the philosophy's rich tapestry, offers a robust framework for navigating the incessant distractions of our digital lives. This ancient yet timeless approach encourages a return to simplicity and presence, helping you cultivate a space where clarity can thrive amidst the chaos of notifications and digital demands.

To integrate Stoic mindfulness into your daily routine, consider the deliberate practice of setting specific times for digital engagement. This could mean scheduling blocks during your day when you check emails, respond to messages, or browse social media. Such structure prevents the constant interruption of your workflow and helps foster a disciplined approach to digital consumption. Imagine beginning your day with a clear schedule where digital interactions are confined to specific hours, liberating vast stretches of your day for deep, uninterrupted work or meaningful face-to-face interactions. This practice aligns with the Stoic virtue of discipline. It enhances your productivity and personal interactions, reinforcing the quality of your professional output and the depth of your relationships.

Practical Strategies for Digital Detox and Managing Information Overload

Implementing digital detoxes and managing information overload with Stoic principles involves setting clear boundaries, practicing mindful consumption, and scheduling regular periods of disconnection. By curating your digital environment—choosing content that enriches rather than overwhelms—you align your technology use with the Stoic virtues of moderation and wisdom. Consider regular digital detoxes like tech-free weekends or daily breaks to reclaim your focus and inner peace. These practices help reduce stress, enhance productivity, and foster a deeper connection with the present moment, reflecting the Stoic ideal of living intentionally.

Mindfulness apps represent a modern tool supporting your Stoic Practice

Unlike many applications designed to capture and monetize your attention, mindfulness apps are uniquely crafted to help you regain control over your focus. These apps often provide guided meditations, breathing exercises, and reminders to pause and reflect, which can be instrumental in cultivating a habit of regular mindfulness. Through these guided practices, you can learn to observe your thoughts and emotions without attachment, gaining the ability to respond to life's challenges with the calm and rational approach that Stoicism advocates.

Whether it's a stressful day at work or a personal challenge that demands your emotional energy, these moments of mindful pause enable you to approach each situation with a clear, composed mind.

Embracing Digital Minimalism

Digital minimalism, a concept that resonates deeply with the Stoic philosophy, advocates for a deliberate approach to technology, focusing on minimizing unnecessary digital distractions that do not serve your essential needs. By adopting a minimalist approach to your digital devices and online presence, you engage in a practice that reduces clutter—both digital and cognitive—and reclaims your time and attention for activities that genuinely align with your values and enhance your life.

Start Digital Minimalism by Reviewing Your Habits

Identify applications and digital activities that consume significant time without adding value to your life. This could be a social media platform you find yourself scrolling through out of habit rather than intention or many apps that send you constant notifications. Once identified, take deliberate steps to reduce or eliminate these distractions—uninstall unnecessary apps, turn off notifications, or even consider setting up a minimalist phone that only includes essential functionalities.

Prioritizing Virtuous Engagements

Beyond simplifying your digital landscape, prioritize activities and engagements that contribute to your personal growth and well-being. Replace the time previously spent on mindless digital consumption with activities that foster your physical, mental, and emotional health—such as reading, exercising, or learning a new skill. This aligns with the Stoic goal of living a virtuous life and enhances your overall well-being, providing a profound sense of fulfillment that fleeting digital distractions cannot offer.

Reclaiming Your Digital Focus

Through these practices, Stoic mindfulness and digital minimalism empower you to navigate the digital age with intention and virtue. By reclaiming your focus and aligning your digital habits with your deepest values, you embody the Stoic ideal of living a purposeful, measured life, one mindful moment at a time.

16.3 The Ethical Use of Technology

Balancing Innovation with Ethics

In the realm of technological innovation, where the pace of development often outstrips the time taken for ethical consideration, the principles of Stoicism provide a necessary grounding. As creators and consumers in this digital age, prioritizing the common good and considering the broader impacts of technological advancements becomes a mandate, not merely a choice. This Stoic approach to technology development emphasizes wisdom, justice, and the pursuit of virtue, advocating for a balance between innovation and ethical responsibility.

Considering Human Flourishing in Technology

When examining the ethical implications of technology development, Stoic philosophy urges us to consider whether these innovations contribute positively to human flourishing and the welfare of society. This perspective is crucial in the decision-making processes of those who develop and deploy technology solutions. For instance, artificial intelligence (AI) development offers profound potential benefits, such as improving healthcare outcomes through more accurate diagnostics or enhancing learning through personalized educational tools. However, these technologies also pose significant ethical challenges, including privacy, surveillance, and the potential for bias in AI algorithms that can perpetuate discrimination.

Wisdom and Justice in Technology

A Stoic approach to these challenges calls for focusing on the virtues of wisdom and justice. In this context, wisdom involves a deep understanding of the potential consequences of technological advancements and the foresight to address these issues proactively. Justice requires equitable distribution of technology benefits and prevention of harm to marginalized groups. For instance, AI developers can incorporate diverse datasets to train algorithms, ensuring that the outputs are not biased against any particular group. Furthermore, transparency about how AI systems make decisions can help build trust and accountability, aligning with Stoic values of honesty and integrity.

Case Study: Ethical Technology Development

Let us consider a case study highlighting the application of Stoic principles in ethical technology development. A tech company aiming to design a new social media platform prioritized user well-being over maximizing engagement—a standard metric that often leads platforms to encourage addictive behaviors. The company applied the Stoic virtues of temperance (moderation) and justice (fairness) by creating features that promote meaningful social interactions rather than frequent, shallow engagement. Additionally, the platform included robust privacy controls that empowered users to understand and manage their data effectively, reflecting the Stoic principle of respecting individual autonomy and integrity.

Long-Term Impact Over Short-Term Gains

This case exemplifies how Stoic principles can guide decisions in technology development to benefit society and avoid harm. It also highlights the importance of considering long-term impacts and the ethical dimensions of technological innovations rather than focusing solely on short-term gains or functionalities. By adhering to these Stoic ideals, developers, and stakeholders in the tech industry can navigate the complex ethical landscape of modern technology with a straightforward, principled approach that promotes the well-being of all.

Ongoing Reflection and Dialogue

Furthermore, the role of technology in society invites continuous reflection and dialogue about its uses and implications. Engaging with diverse perspectives and fostering open discussions about the ethical considerations of technology can further enhance our understanding and implementation of Stoic principles in this field. This collaborative approach enriches the technological community's ethical standards. It ensures that these standards evolve in response to new challenges and insights. In this way, the Stoic commitment to ongoing moral and intellectual growth finds a vital expression in the context of modern technological advances.

Stoic Wisdom in Technological Progress

By grounding technological innovation in Stoic ethics, focusing on the virtues of wisdom, justice, and integrity, we ensure that our technological advancements enhance capabilities and foster a more just, thoughtful, and virtuous society. In this pursuit, the ancient wisdom of Stoicism offers invaluable guidance, reminding us that true progress is measured not by the sophistication of our tools but by the well-being they promote and the ethical standards they uphold.

16.4 Practical Stoic Exercises for the Digital Age

Digital Detox: Disconnect to Reconnect

The rapid pace of technological advancement has deeply enmeshed digital tools into the fabric of our daily lives, bringing unparalleled convenience and new challenges. In this digital age, Stoic philosophy provides a grounding framework, advocating for self-discipline and mindfulness to navigate these challenges effectively. One of the most practical and beneficial Stoic practices adapted for our times is the digital detox. This practice aligns closely with the Stoic emphasis on moderation and self-control, encouraging you to periodically disconnect from digital stimuli and reconnect with your inner self and the natural world.

How to Implement a Digital Detox

Digital detoxes involve deliberate periods of disconnection from all digital devices, providing a respite for your mind and an opportunity to engage in reflective or outdoor activities. For instance, you could designate one weekend each month or a few hours each evening as technology-free, during which you can engage in activities that nourish your soul and body, such as reading, meditating, or taking walks in nature. These periods of disconnection help reduce stress and digital overload and foster greater presence and appreciation for the immediate world around you, enhancing your capacity for mindfulness—a key Stoic value.

Reflecting on Your Relationship with Technology

Moreover, integrating regular digital detoxes into your routine encourages a reflective examination of your relationship with technology. It prompts you to question whether your tech use aligns with your deepest values and life goals or if it merely serves as a distraction from them. Through this introspection, you cultivate a more intentional and disciplined approach to technology that serves your well-being and personal growth rather than detracting from it.

Mindful Technology Use: Engage with Intention

Turning to mindful technology use, Stoicism teaches us to engage with the world intentionally and virtuously. This principle is critically relevant to how you interact with digital technologies. Setting intentional limits on screen time can help you maintain a healthy balance between the digital and physical worlds. You can limit social media use to specific times of the day or use apps to enhance your knowledge and well-being, such as learning a new skill or language.

Curating Your Digital Environment

Furthermore, curating your social media feeds to reflect positive and virtuous content is a direct application of Stoic principles. By following accounts that inspire and educate rather than provoke envy or discontent, you align your digital consumption with Stoic values of wisdom and virtue. This practice improves your emotional and mental environment. It reinforces your commitment to living a Stoic life, even in digital interactions.

Reflecting on Digital Interactions

Lastly, Stoic reflections on digital interactions provide a valuable framework for evaluating how your online behavior aligns with Stoic virtues. Regularly journaling about your digital interactions can enhance your awareness of how well these align with principles such as integrity, kindness, and truthfulness. Reflective prompts such as, "How have my online interactions today reflected my commitment to Stoic virtues?" or "What changes can I make to ensure my digital presence is more aligned with my Stoic practice?" can guide your introspection, fostering a deeper sense of purpose and mindfulness in your digital engagements.

Transforming Digital Habits into Virtuous Practices

By implementing these practices, you not only navigate the digital world with greater wisdom and balance but also cultivate a life that reflects your deepest values and aspirations. The exercises and reflections suggested here are designed to change your digital habits, encouraging a more mindful, intentional, and virtuous interaction with technology. As you incorporate these Stoic exercises into your daily routine, your interactions with technology become more fulfilling, less about consumption, and more about meaningful engagement.

Embodying Stoicism in the Digital Age

In synthesis, with all its innovations and challenges, the digital age calls for a renewed commitment to Stoic principles of discipline, moderation, and mindfulness. By embracing digital detoxes, practicing mindful technology use, and reflecting on your digital interactions, you embody the

Stoic virtues in a modern context, navigating the complexities of digital life with grace and wisdom. As we conclude this exploration of Stoicism in the digital age, let us carry the insights gained here into all aspects of our lives, continually striving for a balance that fosters genuine happiness and well-being.

Reflection Questions:

1. How does Stoic philosophy encourage a mindset of continuous learning and growth?
2. What are the benefits of approaching learning with a Stoic perspective?
3. How can you incorporate the Stoic virtues into your lifelong learning journey?

Journal Prompts:

1. Reflect on a recent learning experience. How can Stoic principles help you enhance your future learning endeavors?
2. Write about a time when you faced a challenge in learning something new. How can applying Stoic practices help you overcome similar challenges in the future?
3. Develop a lifelong learning plan that incorporates Stoic principles. What specific actions will you take to maintain a growth mindset and pursue knowledge continuously?

DEAR READER,

Thank you for choosing *Stoic Philosophy: The Resilient Mindset.* I hope you found it insightful and enriching as you explore the principles of Stoicism in your daily life. Your feedback is invaluable, and I would be grateful if you could take a moment to share your thoughts.

Why Your Review Matters

Your reviews help other readers discover the book and understand its impact. They also provide me with essential feedback that can guide my future writing endeavors. Whether you enjoyed the book or have constructive criticism, every comment counts.

How to Leave a Review

1. **Visit the Amazon Page:** https://mybook.to/StoicPhilosophy
2. Scroll down to the "Customer Reviews" section.
3. Click on "Write a customer review."
4. Share your honest thoughts about the book. Consider discussing:
   - What you found most impactful or insightful.
   - How the book has influenced your understanding of Stoicism.
   - Any practical applications you've experienced.

Or Scan the QR Code Below

Thank you for your support, and I look forward to hearing your thoughts!

Warm regards,

Alex

CONCLUSION

As we draw the curtains on this journey through the timeless wisdom of Stoic philosophy, it's essential to reflect on the path we have traversed together from the ancient teachings of Zeno, Cleanthes, and Chrysippus to the profound impact these ideas have had on figures like Marcus Aurelius and, more contemporarily, on leaders and thinkers across various spheres of life. Stoicism's remarkable evolution and its resurgence in fields such as psychology, leadership, and personal development underscore its enduring relevance and the universal applicability it holds for each of us—whether we are academics, students, professionals, or simply individuals navigating the complexities of modern existence.

The principles of virtue, resilience, and rationality that Stoicism champions are not confined to the pages of history; they are tools that can be wielded in the everyday. These principles empower us to cultivate emotional intelligence, fortify mental toughness, and uphold personal integrity across the diverse scenarios and challenges we encounter. The Stoic practices discussed—morning and evening reflections, intentional journaling, understanding the dichotomy of control, and adopting the view from above—serve as pillars that support a life of mindfulness, purpose, and contentment.

Embracing Stoicism does more than foster personal growth; it propels us towards contributing to a more equitable, empathetic, and understanding society. It teaches us the essence of focusing on what is within our control, accepting the inevitable with grace, and striving to positively influence our immediate environment. This philosophical guide encourages not just self-improvement but societal betterment—a call to action for each of us to embody the virtues we espouse.

The journey with Stoicism does not conclude with the last page of this book. I urge you, the reader, to continually engage with Stoic philosophy—join discussion groups, participate in workshops, and delve into the seminal texts that have carried these teachings through millennia. These steps will enrich your understanding and enhance your ability to integrate Stoic principles into daily life.

Continuing Your Stoic Journey

Now that you've explored the timeless wisdom of Stoicism and its application to modern life, I encourage you to integrate these insights into your daily routine. Approach life's inevitable ups and downs with a balanced perspective, find joy in the simple moments, and lead with purpose and integrity. Let Stoic practices guide you as you navigate life's trials and triumphs.

Reflecting on my journey with Stoicism, I'm reminded of the profound transformation it has brought into my life—instilling peace, resilience, and deep fulfillment. My hope is that you, too, will experience similar transformative effects as you apply these age-old yet incredibly relevant teachings.

Thank you for joining me on this enlightening exploration of Stoic philosophy. Your commitment to personal growth and societal improvement through Stoicism is truly commendable. As you continue on your path of learning and reflection, may you find the strength, wisdom, and tranquility that this philosophy so generously offers.

Wishing you a journey of continuous learning, reflection, and fulfillment with Stoicism.

Final Reflections

1. How has your understanding of Stoic philosophy evolved throughout this book?
2. What are the key Stoic principles that resonate most with you, and how can you apply them in your daily life?
3. How can you inspire others to practice Stoicism through your example and actions?

Journal Prompts:

1. Reflect on your journey with Stoicism so far. What changes have you noticed in your mindset and behavior?
2. Write a letter to your future self, describing how you plan to continue practicing Stoicism and the goals you hope to achieve.
3. Create a personal Stoic manifesto. Outline the key principles you will commit to following and the actions you will take to live a virtuous and meaningful life.

APPENDIX:

ACCESSING FREE ADDITIONAL RESOURCES

We are pleased to offer a comprehensive set of free appendices to further support your journey into Stoicism with *Stoic Philosophy - The Resilient Mindset.* These resources include worksheets, templates, case studies, and curated reading materials designed to enhance your understanding and application of Stoic principles.

To access them, simply click the link below or scan the QR code. You will receive an email with a link to access the appendices, including free templates, diagrams, and more—everything you need to deepen your engagement with Stoic wisdom.

Click here

By entering your email, you'll gain access to valuable resources and updates that will enhance your leadership journey with tools and insights to support your growth.

I'm also excited to announce that the final book in this series, ***Beyond the Surface: Deep Leadership, Stoic Insight, and Daily Clarity***, is due out shortly. This companion book offers daily Stoic Meditations, allowing you to engage with whichever meditation resonates with you each day, guided by an inner source of wisdom.

In addition, I've launched a YouTube channel that includes a private playlist available exclusively to those who have purchased this book. This playlist features recorded video meditations and insights into Stoic philosophy, providing a deeper, more immersive experience to complement your reading. It's a valuable resource for anyone looking to incorporate Stoic principles into their daily life.

YouTube Channel

Thank you for allowing me to be a part of your journey. Your growth, resilience, and pursuit of wisdom are what make this endeavor worthwhile. I look forward to continuing this journey with you in spirit, as you forge ahead with the courage and insight that Stoic philosophy inspires.

With gratitude and respect,

Alex

REFERENCES:

Stoicism. (n.d.). *Stanford Encyclopedia of Philosophy*. Retrieved February 15, 2024, from https://plato.stanford.edu/entries/stoicism/#:~=The%20Stoic%20school%20was%20founded,Academy%20and%20the%20Megarian%20School

Stoicism and its influence on Roman life and thought. (n.d.). Retrieved January 20, 2024, from https://www.jstor.org/stable/3289820

Marcus Aurelius. (n.d.). *Stanford Encyclopedia of Philosophy*. Retrieved March 5, 2024, from https://plato.stanford.edu/entries/marcus-aurelius/

Roman Stoicism | Overview, beliefs & virtues. (n.d.). Retrieved June 10, 2024, from https://study.com/academy/lesson/stoicism-understanding-roman-moral-philosophy.html#:~=Roman%20Virtues%20vs.,-Stoicism's%20Virtues&text=Traditional%20Roman%20virtues%20were%20greater,the%20will%20of%20the%20gods

Marcus Aurelius | Biography, meditations, & facts. (n.d.). *Britannica*. Retrieved April 22, 2024, from https://www.britannica.com/biography/Marcus-Aurelius-Roman-emperor#:~=Marcus%20Aurelius%20came%20from%20a,emperor%20Antoninus%20Pius's%20daughter

Marcus Aurelius: The Stoic who led with grace. (n.d.). Retrieved May 11, 2024, from https://www.globalleadersinstitute.org/blog-post/marcus-aurelius-the-stoic-who-taught-us-to-lead-with-grace/

Robertson, D. (2017, March 1). Marcus Aurelius: The education of a philosopher. Retrieved January 5, 2024, from https://donaldrobertson.name/2017/03/01/marcus-aurelius-the-education-of-a-philosopher/

Meditations study guide - Marcus Aurelius. (n.d.). Retrieved February 28, 2024, from https://www.litcharts.com/lit/meditations

Marcus Aurelius. (n.d.). *Stanford Encyclopedia of Philosophy*. Retrieved March 7, 2024, from https://plato.stanford.edu/entries/marcus-aurelius/

Del Testa, D. (n.d.). Marcus Aurelius | Roman emperor and philosopher 121–180. In *Encyclopedia of World History* (pp. 117). Retrieved May 18, 2024, from https://www.taylorfrancis.com/chapters/edit/10.4324/9781315063706-117/marcus-aurelius-david-del-testa

Marcomannic Wars: Conflict that challenged Rome. (n.d.). Retrieved April 9, 2024, from https://roman-empire.net/army/marcomannic-wars/

Robertson, D. (n.d.). Marcus Aurelius on stoicism and leadership. Retrieved June 25, 2024, from https://donaldrobertson.substack.com/p/marcus-aurelius-on-stoicism-and-leadership-9bcd3854834f

Meditations by Marcus Aurelius: Book summary, key lessons. (n.d.). Retrieved January 30, 2024, from https://dailystoic.com/meditations-marcus-aurelius/#:~=Five%20of%20the%20main%20themes,and%20fully%20accepting%20its%20course

What stoic philosophers can teach us about grief. (n.d.). Retrieved February 13, 2024, from https://lithub.com/what-stoic-philosophers-can-teach-us-about-grief/

How to plan your day like Marcus Aurelius. (n.d.). Retrieved June 14, 2024, from https://dailystoic.com/marcus-aurelius-daily-habits/

Stoicism and pain management: 4 techniques practiced. (n.d.). Retrieved May 6, 2024, from https://dailystoic.com/stoicism-and-pain-management/

Marcus Aurelius a persecutor? | Harvard Theological Review. (n.d.). Retrieved April 28, 2024, from https://www.cambridge.org/core/journals/harvard-theological-review/article/marcus-aurelius-a-persecutor/E8F76CB327530CF310251FDFCC1ADDF2

Emperors and empire. Marcus Aurelius and Commodus. (n.d.). Retrieved January 10, 2024, from https://www.degruyter.com/document/doi/10.1515/9783110446661-015/html?lang=en

Epictetus, stoicism, and slavery. (n.d.). *University of Colorado Boulder*. Retrieved February 1, 2024, from https://scholar.colorado.edu/downloads/

fn106z451#:~=While%20the%20Stoics%20did%20not,hundred%20 years%20of%20Roman%20history

Women and stoic ethics in early modern England. (n.d.). Retrieved April 15, 2024, from https://compass.onlinelibrary.wiley.com/doi/full/10.1111/phc3.12933

Directing your focus with stoicism and CBT. (n.d.). *Psychology Today*. Retrieved June 2, 2024, from https://www.psychologytoday.com/us/blog/beyond-school-walls/202306/directing-your-focus-with-stoicism-and-cbt#:~=The%20intersection%20of%20Stoicism%2C%20an,over%20 their%20thoughts%20and%20actions

Reading Marcus Aurelius's meditations with a modern perspective. (n.d.). *Oxford University Press Blog*. Retrieved March 11, 2024, from https://blog.oup.com/2014/10/marcus-aurelius-meditation-modern-perspective/

Mindfulness vs stoicism: Philosophy as a way of life. (n.d.). *MindOwl*. Retrieved January 25, 2024, from https://mindowl.org/mindfulness-vs-stoicism/#:~=Stoicism%20and%20mindfulness%20come%20 from,focuses%20on%20awareness%20without%20judgment

8 stoic principles for leadership. (n.d.). Retrieved February 23, 2024, from https://www.tristanahumada.com/blog/8-stoic-principles-for-leadership

Marcus Aurelius and modern psychological therapy. (n.d.). Retrieved March 22, 2024, from https://timboatswain.wixsite.com/website/post/marcus-aurelius-and-modern-psychological-therapy

How to use stoicism to build emotional resilience. (n.d.). Retrieved May 28, 2024, from https://orionphilosophy.com/stoicism-and-emotional-resilience/

Stoicism for conflict resolution: Use stoic philosophy to resolve conflicts. (n.d.). Retrieved June 12, 2024, from https://www.stoicsimple.com/stoicism-for-conflict-resolution-use-stoic-philosophy-to-resolve-conflicts/

Stoicism and environmental ethics: Living in harmony with nature. (n.d.). Retrieved January 17, 2024, from https://medium.com/@stoicminds.channel/stoicism-and-environmental-ethics-living-in-harmony-with-nature-a28b5ff76654

Marcus Aurelius. (n.d.). *Stanford Encyclopedia of Philosophy*. Retrieved February 6, 2024, from https://plato.stanford.edu/entries/marcus-aurelius/

Stoicism and Confucianism: A comparison. (n.d.). *Medium*. Retrieved March 10, 2024, from https://medium.com/the-philosophers-stone/stoicism-and-confucianism-a-comparison-e9ebc24dee51

What is stoicism? A definition & 9 stoic exercises to get started. (n.d.). *Daily Stoic*. Retrieved May 9, 2024, from https://dailystoic.com/what-is-stoicism-a-definition-3-stoic-exercises-to-get-you-started/

Modern stoicism and its usefulness in fostering resilience. (n.d.). Retrieved April 18, 2024, from https://www.crisisjournal.org/api/v1/articles/33608-modern-stoicism-and-its-usefulness-in-fostering-resilience.pdf

FEMA. (2008). *Rebuilding After the Storm: Greensburg, Kansas, Leads the Way in Sustainability.* Federal Emergency Management Agency. Retrieved from FEMA.gov.

National Geographic. (2008). *Greensburg: The Green Town Reborn from a Natural Disaster.* [Documentary Series]. National Geographic Channel. Retrieved from Natihttps://www.nationalgeographic.com/tv

Johnson, K. (2007, October 19). *In Tornado's Wake, Greensburg, Kansas, Imagines a Green Future.* The New York Times. Retrieved from nytimes.com

www.ingramcontent.com/pod-product-compliance
Lightning Source LLC
LaVergne TN
LVHW050542160826
845677LV00011B/2144

* 9 7 9 8 2 2 7 8 4 6 3 8 9 *